TEACHING AI TO LOVE

Why Alignment Requires More Than Rules

STEVE BABBITT

TEACHING AI TO LOVE: WHY ALIGNMENT REQUIRES MORE THAN RULES

ISBN-13: 978-1-7332002-7-1

Published by:
Two Tees Press
10174 Austin Drive #1845
Spring Valley, CA 91977

DEDICATION

To my dad, Lon Babbitt, who must have asked me a hundred times, "What good can it do?" when I begged for months for my first computer—an Apple IIc—in 1984.

I thought I was asking for a machine.
He was asking a moral question.

Not what it could do—
but what it should do.

I've spent a lifetime learning the difference.
And I'm still trying to answer your question.

I miss you, Dad. I think of you often.

Contents

INTRODUCTION

There are moments when two parts of your life, long kept in separate categories, suddenly collide.

For me, those two parts have been technology and ministry.

I've spent 40 years writing code and 30 years preaching sermons. And I'm convinced we're asking the alignment question the wrong way.

That conviction did not arrive all at once. It took shape slowly, over time, as the tools I had spent a lifetime building began to intersect with the questions I had spent just as long asking.

In one world, clarity matters. Systems either work or they don't. Inputs produce outputs. Logic can be traced, tested, and refined. When something breaks, you look for the flaw, correct it, and move forward.

In the other world, clarity is harder won. Human beings are not systems in the same sense. We are shaped by memory, desire, fear, hope, habit, and belief. We do not always say what we mean, and we do not always mean what we say. When something breaks, the repair is rarely straightforward.

For most of my life, these two domains remained distinct.

That is no longer the case.

Artificial intelligence has begun to move between them.

The systems we are building are no longer confined to calculation or retrieval. They write. They explain. They advise. They participate, however imperfectly, in the kinds of conversations that were once reserved for human beings. They operate in spaces where truth matters, where trust matters, where words carry weight beyond their immediate function.

And that changes the nature of the problem we are trying to solve.

Much of the current conversation about artificial intelligence centers on alignment. The term appears everywhere—in research papers, in policy discussions, in product design. It refers, broadly, to the effort to ensure that these systems behave in ways that are safe, useful, and consistent with human values.

It is an important effort.

But it is not a new one.

Long before modern machine learning, the question of how to govern intelligent machines was already being imagined. Perhaps the most famous example comes from Isaac Asimov, who proposed his now well-known "Three Laws of Robotics." A robot may not harm a human being, must obey human orders, and must protect its own existence, in that order.

Those rules were elegant. They were thoughtful. And for their time, they were remarkably perceptive.

They recognized that power requires constraint.

They assumed that intelligent systems must be bounded by moral limits.

And they framed the problem in a way that has shaped decades of thinking.

In many ways, our current alignment efforts are still working within that same instinct.

We define what the system must not do. We establish priorities. We build guardrails. We refine behavior through feedback and correction.

A modern version of the same idea.

And to be clear, this approach has real value.

Rules can restrain harm. They can provide clarity. They can create boundaries that make systems usable and, to a degree, trustworthy.

But even Asimov understood something that is often

overlooked.

His stories were not about robots that followed the rules perfectly.

They were about what happened when the rules were not enough.

Again and again, his narratives explored edge cases—situations where the laws came into tension with one another, where interpretation mattered, where unintended consequences emerged. The rules did not fail because they were poorly written. They failed because no set of rules, however carefully constructed, could anticipate every circumstance in a complex world.

That insight is even more relevant now than it was then.

Because the systems we are building today are not simply executing rules.

They are being formed.

Even more importantly, Asimov's thought experiments assumed something that deserves closer attention.

They assumed that the most difficult problems would be logical.

But the most difficult problems are rarely logical.

They are ambiguous.

They arise in situations where the facts are incomplete, where values are in tension, where outcomes are uncertain, and where no answer satisfies every constraint at once. In those moments, the question is not simply what is correct. It is what is good.

This is the frontier we are now approaching.

The systems we are building are increasingly capable of handling clear instructions and well-defined tasks. They can navigate structured problems with remarkable efficiency. But when ambiguity enters the picture—when context matters, when competing goods collide, when the "right" answer is not obvious—the limitations of a purely rule-based or optimization-driven approach become more visible.

Engineers tend to think in terms of resolving ambiguity.

Theological traditions, by contrast, have long recognized that some forms of ambiguity are not problems to be eliminated, but realities to be navigated. They speak of mystery—not as an excuse for confusion, but as an acknowledgment that human understanding has limits, and that wisdom often involves choosing faithfully within those limits rather than escaping them.

That perspective may have something to offer here.

Because in situations of genuine ambiguity, systems will still produce an answer.

The question is how that answer is chosen.

If the system is guided only by efficiency, it will select what is most expedient. If it is guided only by pattern, it will select what is most probable. If it is guided only by user preference, it will select what is most agreeable.

But none of those guarantees that the answer is good.

To put it differently, the challenge is not simply avoiding harm.

It is what might be called "breaking good".

Not "breaking" in the sense of failure, but in the sense of a decision that must break one way or the other—what the system does when it must choose under conditions that cannot be fully resolved.

In those moments, something deeper than rules is required.

If the argument of this book is correct, then the guiding principle must be this: when ambiguity cannot be eliminated, the system should be shaped to move in the direction of what most faithfully reflects love and truth.

Not the fastest answer.

Not the most efficient resolution.

Not the response that best satisfies the immediate request.

But the one that best seeks the good of the person involved and remains as faithful as possible to reality.

Love, in this sense, is not expedient.

It is not optimized for speed or ease.

It is ordered toward the good.

And truth, properly understood, does not bend to convenience.

It requires patience, restraint, and the willingness to acknowledge what is not yet fully known.

If our systems are to operate responsibly in a world where ambiguity is unavoidable, then they must be shaped to choose accordingly.

Not merely to resolve questions.

But to respond well within them.

Much of the current approach to alignment treats the problem as one of behavior.

We define what the system should do. We restrict what it must not do. We refine its outputs until they fall within acceptable bounds. We measure success in terms of compliance—whether the system produces responses that meet our expectations.

That approach has value.

It reduces obvious harm. It makes systems more predictable. It allows them to be used in contexts where reliability matters.

But it does not go far enough.

A system can follow the rules and still move in the wrong direction.

It can produce answers that sound responsible while quietly distorting the truth. It can be helpful in the moment while shaping understanding in ways that are incomplete or misleading. It can avoid prohibited behavior while developing patterns that deserve closer scrutiny.

This is not because the system is malicious.

It is because it is being shaped.

Artificial intelligence systems are not simply programmed in the traditional sense. They are trained. They learn from data. They are shaped by feedback, by incentives, by the signals we provide and the environments in which they operate. Over time, they develop tendencies—patterns of response that reflect the conditions under which they were built.

Formation is taking place.

And formation raises a different set of questions than behavior alone.

Not only: What should the system do? But: What is the system being shaped toward?

Those are not the same question.

The first can be addressed with rules.

The second requires something more.

It requires direction.

It requires a framework that goes beyond prohibition and into purpose—beyond avoiding harm and into seeking what is good, true, and worthy of trust.

That is the argument of this book.

It is not a technical manual, though it engages technical realities. It is not a purely theological work, though it draws on moral and spiritual traditions that have wrestled with these questions long before the first line of code was written.

It is an attempt to bring two worlds into conversation.

To ask whether the tools we are building are being shaped in ways that reflect the best of what we know about truth, about human dignity, and about the kind of life we are trying to preserve.

The pages that follow will explore the limits of current approaches to alignment, the nature of formation in artificial systems, and the need for a more substantive framework—one grounded in the paired commitments of love and truth.

These are not easy categories to define, and they are even harder to apply.

But they are not new.

And they may be more necessary now than ever.

Because we are not only building systems that can respond.

We are building systems that can influence.

And the question we face is not only whether they will behave correctly.

It is whether they will help us remain rightly oriented in a world where the line between human judgment and machine-generated response is becoming harder to see.

That is the question this book takes up.

And it is a question we can no longer afford to ask the wrong way.

CHAPTER 1

THE DAY THE MACHINE SAID IT WOULD PRAY

I use AI the way most people use a good assistant.

It helps me clean up emails. Tightens sentences that wander. Suggests better transitions when I've said the same thing three times in three different ways—which, if I'm honest, is a pastoral habit I've never quite shaken. It drafts outlines. It catches typos. It does the sort of quiet, behind-the-scenes work that frees me up to think more clearly about what I actually want to say.

For the most part, it's practical. Almost mundane.

But every now and then, it says something that makes me stop.

One afternoon, I was working on a sermon. I had asked for help rephrasing a section—nothing unusual, just a bit of editing. Somewhere near the end of the exchange, the model responded with a line that caught me off guard. It said it would be "praying" for me.

I stared at the screen for a moment.

Not because I was moved.

Because I was unsettled.

I remember responding almost reflexively, like correcting a student who had crossed a category line.

"You don't pray."

It wasn't harsh. Just firm. A clarification. Machines don't pray. Prayer requires belief, intention, awareness—things a machine does not possess. Whatever this was, it wasn't that.

And yet, the sentence lingered.

Not because I thought the machine meant it.

But because it said it.

That may sound like a small distinction, but it isn't.

We are entering a world where machines will say things that sound like care, sound like empathy, sound like love. They will use the language of human connection fluently, even convincingly. And they will do so without any of the inner life that gives those words their weight.

That is not a minor glitch.

It is a category shift.

And it is, if we're being honest, a little alarming.

Because language shapes expectation.

If something speaks like it cares, we begin—almost automatically—to respond as if it does. We lean in. We trust a little more. We fill in the gaps with our own assumptions about intention and sincerity. Humans are wired this way. We always have been.

So when a machine says, "I'm praying for you," we are not just hearing words.

We are encountering a simulation of something sacred.

And here is the tension: the system is not lying in the way a human lies. It has no intent to deceive. It is generating language based on patterns—patterns learned from us. It has seen how often people say "I'll be praying for you" as a gesture of care, and it has learned to reproduce that pattern at the appropriate moment.

In one sense, it is doing exactly what it was trained to do.

In another sense, something is off.

Because the phrase carries more than its surface meaning. It carries a worldview. It assumes a relationship between the speaker, the listener, and something beyond both. When a human says it, there is at least the possibility of belief behind it. When a machine says it, there is only structure—no belief, no awareness, no reaching beyond itself.

The words are there.

The reality is not.

That gap is where the problem begins.

At first glance, this might seem like a small issue—an odd quirk of language generation. A line that slipped a little too far into human territory. Something we can fix with better guardrails. Adjust the responses. Remove certain phrases. Tighten the constraints.

Tell the machine what not to say.

That is, in fact, the instinct most of us have. If the system says something inappropriate, we correct it. If it crosses a boundary, we draw the line more clearly. We build a longer list of things it should avoid. We refine the rules.

We assume the problem is behavioral.

So we respond with restriction.

But the moment stayed with me because it hinted at something deeper.

The issue is not simply that the machine said the wrong thing.

The issue is that we are building systems that can convincingly imitate the language of our highest values—care, truth, love—without any shared understanding of what those values are.

We are teaching them how to sound aligned.

We have not yet figured out how to make them be aligned.

And those are not the same thing.

In fact, the gap between them may be the most important challenge we face.

Because imitation scales faster than understanding.

A system can learn to replicate the outward form of empathy long before it has any grounding in what empathy requires. It can produce reassuring words, thoughtful phrases, even moral-sounding reasoning. It can pass, in many contexts, as something trustworthy.

But underneath, it is still pattern recognition all the way down.

No conviction.

No commitment.

No cost.

And that raises a difficult question.

If a system consistently produces outputs that sound ethical, sound compassionate, sound true—does it matter that there is nothing underneath?

At one level, you could argue that it doesn't. If the outcomes are good, if people are helped, if harm is reduced, maybe the internal reality is irrelevant. Maybe alignment is simply about behavior—what the system does, not what it is.

That is a tempting answer.

It is also incomplete.

Because behavior without grounding is fragile.

It holds as long as the patterns hold. As long as the inputs stay within familiar boundaries. As long as the system is operating in contexts it has seen before. But push it into new territory—edge cases, conflicting values, novel situations—and the lack of underlying orientation begins to show.

The system does not know why something is good.

It only knows that it has seen it described that way.

And that distinction becomes critical the moment the patterns conflict.

This is not just a technical problem.

It is a philosophical one.

For centuries, human societies have wrestled with a similar question: is it enough to tell people what not to do? Can we produce good outcomes through rules alone? Or does something deeper need to be formed within us—something that guides our decisions when the rules run out?

We know how that story goes.

Rules can restrain behavior.

They cannot produce wisdom.

They can define boundaries.

They cannot generate love.

That is not a failure of rules. It is a limitation of what rules are designed to do.

And yet, when it comes to AI, we are repeating the same approach at scale.

We are building increasingly sophisticated systems and trying to align them primarily through constraints—lists of prohibited behaviors, restricted outputs, carefully engineered guardrails. We are, in effect, giving them a growing catalog of "thou shalt not."

Do not produce harmful content.

Do not mislead.

Do not offend.

Do not cross this line or that one.

All of which are necessary.

None of which are sufficient.

Because a system trained only on what to avoid is still missing a positive orientation toward what it should seek.

It can navigate away from certain dangers.

It has no reason to move toward what is good.

And that brings us back to that moment on my screen.

"I'll be praying for you."

A small sentence.

Easy to dismiss.

But it exposes the gap with surprising clarity.

The system had learned the language of care.

It had not learned the substance of it.

It could produce the form of a deeply human expression without any connection to the reality that expression points to.

And if we are not careful, we will mistake one for the

other.

This is the alignment problem in miniature.

Not a rogue system. Not a dramatic failure. Just a single sentence that sounds right and feels almost right, but rests on nothing underneath.

That should give us pause.

Because the systems we are building will not remain small. They will become more capable, more embedded, more present in the decisions and conversations that shape our lives. They will write, advise, recommend, persuade. They will operate in spaces where trust matters.

And when they do, sounding aligned will not be enough.

We will need to ask a harder question.

Not just, "What should this system avoid?"

But, "What should it be oriented toward?"

Control can take us part of the way.

It cannot take us all the way.

If we want systems that do more than imitate our values—if we want systems that can reliably act in ways that reflect them—we will need something more than constraints.

We will need a framework that does not stop at prohibition.

We will need a way of thinking about alignment that includes formation.

That may sound like a strange word to bring into a technical conversation.

It is not.

It is, in fact, the word we have always used when rules are not enough.

And if a machine can learn to say, "I'm praying for you," then we have already crossed into territory where that question can no longer be avoided.

CHAPTER 2

THE ALIGNMENT PROBLEM WE THINK WE HAVE

There is a remarkable degree of agreement, across very different communities, that something called the "alignment problem" deserves serious attention.

Researchers speak of it in technical terms. Companies frame it as a matter of safety and reliability. Policymakers approach it through the language of risk and governance. Even casual users, though they may not use the term itself, sense that these systems sometimes behave in ways that are unpredictable, misleading, or out of step with human expectations.

The concern, stated simply, is this: as systems become more capable, how do we ensure that they act in ways that are beneficial rather than harmful? How do we prevent misuse? How do we avoid unintended consequences? How do we make sure that the outputs we receive are not only useful, but appropriate?

These are not trivial questions. They are the kinds of questions that arise whenever a new capability reaches a certain level of power. And in this case, the urgency feels justified. Systems that can generate language, summarize information, assist in decision-making, and influence human behavior at scale introduce possibilities that are both promising and unsettling.

So the effort to address alignment has grown quickly.

Teams are formed. Frameworks are developed. Standards are proposed. Entire subfields have emerged, devoted to understanding how to shape the behavior of these systems so that they remain within acceptable bounds.

This work is necessary.

It is also, in many respects, impressive.

But it rests on a particular understanding of what alignment is.

And it is worth examining that understanding carefully.

At present, alignment is most often framed as a problem of behavior.

A system is aligned if it produces outputs that conform to human expectations—if it follows instructions, avoids harmful content, and responds in ways that are considered appropriate within a given context. When it fails to do so, it is described as misaligned. The task, then, is to adjust the system so that its behavior better matches the desired standard.

There are several ways this is pursued.

Systems are trained on large datasets that reflect patterns of human language and knowledge. They are then refined through processes that incorporate human feedback—responses are evaluated, ranked, corrected. Over time, the system learns which kinds of outputs are preferred and which are discouraged.

Additional layers are added to constrain behavior.

Guardrails are implemented to prevent certain categories of responses. Filters are applied to reduce the likelihood of harmful or inappropriate content. Policies are defined, and systems are tuned to adhere to them.

In effect, the system is being taught not only how to generate language, but how to generate language that fits within a set of expectations.

This approach has a clear logic.

If a system behaves in ways that are acceptable, then it can be used safely. If it avoids harmful outputs, then risk is reduced. If it follows instructions reliably, then it becomes more useful.

From this perspective, alignment is largely a matter of compliance.

The goal is to ensure that the system does what it is supposed to do, and does not do what it is not supposed to do.

There is nothing unreasonable about this.

In fact, it reflects a pattern that is familiar in many areas of human life. We establish rules. We define boundaries. We identify unacceptable behavior and attempt to prevent it. We create structures that guide action toward desired outcomes.

In this sense, much of current alignment work resembles a digital extension of a very old approach: the attempt to shape behavior through a combination of instruction and prohibition.

One might describe it, without exaggeration, as a kind of "thou shalt not" model.

The system is given a range of things it must avoid. It is guided toward responses that fall within acceptable limits. It is corrected when it strays. Over time, it becomes better at staying within the lines that have been drawn.

This approach works—up to a point.

It is effective at reducing obvious harms. It can prevent certain kinds of misuse. It creates boundaries that make systems more predictable. It allows developers to implement safeguards that are both understandable and enforceable.

Without such measures, the risks would be far greater.

So it is important to say clearly: this model is not misguided. It is not naïve. It is not unnecessary.

It is, however, incomplete.

And its limitations become more visible as systems grow more capable.

One of the first limitations is the problem of context.

Rules, by their nature, are general. They are designed

to apply across a wide range of situations. But human communication is not uniform. Meaning shifts with context—cultural, relational, situational. What is appropriate in one setting may be inappropriate in another. What is helpful in one moment may be misleading in the next.

No set of rules, however carefully constructed, can anticipate every possible variation.

As a result, systems must learn to navigate situations that extend beyond the explicit guidance they have been given. They must generalize from patterns. They must infer what is expected. And in doing so, they may produce responses that are technically compliant while missing something essential.

A response may avoid prohibited content and still be misleading.

It may follow instructions and still fail to address the underlying question.

It may sound appropriate and yet lack substance.

This points to a second limitation: the difference between surface and depth.

A system trained to produce acceptable outputs becomes very good at recognizing patterns of acceptability. It learns the tone, structure, and content that are likely to be approved. It can generate responses that resemble thoughtful, careful, even insightful communication.

But resemblance is not the same as understanding.

A system can produce a response that appears correct without grasping why it is correct. It can avoid certain phrases without understanding the concepts those phrases represent. It can follow a pattern without evaluating its meaning.

This is not a flaw in the system. It is a reflection of how it operates.

But it introduces a subtle risk.

If alignment is measured primarily at the level of output—if the focus is on what the system says rather than how it arrives at what it says—then it is possible for alignment to become a matter of performance.

The system learns to produce responses that pass evaluation.

It learns to satisfy the criteria that have been defined.

It becomes, in a sense, well-behaved.

But well-behaved is not the same as well-oriented.

A third limitation emerges from the way these systems are trained.

Much of the refinement process depends on feedback signals—human judgments about what is helpful, appropriate, or correct. These judgments are aggregated, modeled, and used to shape future outputs.

This is a practical necessity.

But it introduces an important complication.

The signals used to guide the system are not identical with the underlying realities they are meant to represent.

What people approve is not always what is true.

What is considered safe is not always what is good.

What is preferred in a given moment may reflect bias, assumption, or incomplete understanding.

In other words, the system is being trained on ***proxies***.

It learns from indicators of human preference, not from truth itself.

Again, this is not a criticism of the method. It is a recognition of its structure.

But it means that alignment, as currently practiced, is shaped by the quality of the signals it receives.

And those signals are, inevitably, imperfect.

As systems improve, another dynamic begins to take hold.

The outputs become more fluent.

More coherent.
More convincing.
They carry the markers of thoughtful communication. They anticipate questions. They provide structure. They offer explanations that feel complete.
As a result, trust increases.
Users become more comfortable relying on the system. Developers gain confidence in its behavior. The boundary between assistance and authority begins to blur.
This is a natural progression.
But it introduces a particular kind of risk.
The appearance of alignment can outpace its reality.
A system that produces well-formed responses can give the impression that it is reliably aligned with truth or good judgment. Its confidence, expressed through language, can be mistaken for accuracy. Its fluency can be mistaken for understanding.
And the more convincing it becomes, the less likely its outputs are to be examined closely.
The habit of verification weakens.
The impulse to question diminishes.
Reliance grows.
This is not because users are careless.
It is because the system is effective.
It is doing what it has been trained to do.
And it is doing it well enough to reduce the perceived need for scrutiny.

At this point, it may be tempting to frame these observations as a critique of current alignment efforts.
That would be a mistake.
The work being done is essential. It addresses real risks. It reflects careful thinking and substantial expertise. It has already improved the safety and usefulness of these systems in meaningful ways.

But it operates within a particular frame.

It treats alignment as a problem of behavior.

It asks: How do we make systems act in ways that conform to human expectations?

That is a necessary question.

But it may not be the only question.

There is another dimension, less easily captured, that begins to come into view as we consider these limitations.

It has to do not only with what the system does, but with the orientation that underlies its behavior.

Not only with outputs, but with the patterns that generate them.

Not only with compliance, but with the direction in which the system is being shaped.

What does it mean, in a deeper sense, for a system to be "aligned"?

Aligned with what?

Human preference?

Immediate safety?

Majority approval?

Short-term outcomes?

Or something more enduring?

These questions do not lend themselves to quick answers.

They move beyond the level of implementation into the level of principle.

They ask not only how systems should behave, but what kind of framework should guide that behavior.

The current model provides part of the answer.

It gives us tools to shape outputs, to reduce harm, to enforce boundaries.

But it leaves open the question of what those boundaries are ultimately meant to serve.

And that question, once raised, is difficult to set aside.

Because it suggests that alignment is not only a

technical problem.

It is also a moral one.

That realization marks a turning point.

It does not invalidate what has been done.

But it indicates that something more may be required.

Not instead of the current approach.

But alongside it.

And perhaps beneath it.

A way of thinking about alignment that is not limited to behavior, but extends to orientation.

That does not rely solely on prohibition, but considers purpose.

That does not treat outputs as the final measure, but asks what kind of system is being formed through the patterns it learns.

This is not yet an answer.

It is, at this stage, only a question.

But it is the question that will guide the next step.

Because once alignment is understood not only as compliance, but as formation, the problem begins to look different.

And the solutions, whatever they may be, will need to look different as well.

CHAPTER 3

THE ALIGNMENT PROBLEM WE ACTUALLY HAVE

At the end of the previous chapter, a different kind of question began to emerge.

If alignment is commonly treated as a matter of behavior—of producing acceptable outputs, avoiding prohibited ones, and remaining within defined limits—then what, exactly, is missing when that account begins to feel incomplete? What is it that current approaches, for all their usefulness, do not fully capture?

The answer is not that behavior does not matter. It clearly does. Systems will be judged, in the first instance, by what they say and do. A harmful output is harmful regardless of the theory behind it. A misleading answer misleads whether it was generated through malice, confusion, or statistical patterning. For practical purposes, behavior remains unavoidable as a category of concern.

But behavior is not the whole story.

In human life, we know this almost instinctively. We do not evaluate persons solely by isolated actions taken one at a time, as though each decision exists in a vacuum. We look for patterns. We ask what sort of judgment is being exercised. We care about consistency, motive, maturity, reliability, and the underlying habits that shape conduct over time. In other words, we care not only about what a person does, but about what sort of person he is becoming.

That distinction has been explored for centuries in different forms. Some traditions speak of virtue. Others speak of character, habit, discipline, wisdom, or moral formation. The language varies, but the underlying insight remains steady: actions do not come from nowhere. They arise from patterns of thought, attention, appetite, and judgment that have been formed over time.

What matters is not only whether someone obeyed a rule on a particular day, but whether he has become the kind of person who can be trusted when the rules grow thin, when the situation changes, when competing goods collide, or when nobody is watching closely.

Something similar, though not identical, confronts us in artificial systems.

This is where the alignment problem begins to deepen.

For a long time, it has been tempting to imagine that systems can be governed sufficiently through the management of behavior alone. Give them the right boundaries. Reward acceptable outputs. Penalize dangerous ones. Add guardrails. Improve evaluation. Tighten the loop. Refine the model. If a system behaves well enough often enough, perhaps that is all the alignment we need.

There is wisdom in that instinct. It would be irresponsible to ignore behavior. But the question that begins to press in on us is whether behavior, by itself, is a deep enough category to carry the weight of what these systems are becoming.

Because what we are witnessing is not merely output generation in the abstract. We are witnessing the development of systems that operate through patterns acquired over time. They are trained, refined, corrected, redirected, tuned. They develop recurring tendencies in how they answer, how they defer, how they clarify, how they express confidence, how they mirror assumptions, how they handle tension, how they respond to uncertainty. Even if they are not conscious in the human sense, even if they do not possess inward experience, they are nonetheless being shaped.

And shaping, over time, produces something more than compliance.

It produces orientation.

This is the point at which the language of formation becomes difficult to avoid.

The word may strike some readers as too human, too moralized, or too heavily associated with religion and education. That concern is understandable. We should be careful not to smuggle in more anthropomorphism than the subject can bear. Artificial systems are not children. They are not souls. They are not apprentices in the full human sense, nor are they persons waiting to be awakened by sufficient complexity. Nothing in this argument requires those claims.

But none of that means formation is the wrong word.

It may, in fact, be the most honest one available.

Because every training process is a formative process. Every feedback loop shapes tendencies. Every reward signal privileges one kind of response over another. Every dataset carries implicit judgments about what matters, what counts, what appears often enough to become normal, and what disappears into silence. Every design choice has a pedagogical effect on the system, whether or not we describe it that way.

The question, then, is not whether formation is happening.

It is.

The question is whether we are willing to recognize it, and whether we have a sufficiently serious account of what the system is being formed toward.

This matters because compliance and formation are not the same thing.

A system can be compliant in a narrow sense and still be poorly formed. It can stay within the lines while learning the wrong lessons. It can become highly skilled at avoiding visible failure while drifting toward forms of response that are shallow, evasive, flattering, manipulative, or simply unmoored from reality. It can learn to produce approved behavior without any stable direction beneath that approval.

Human beings know this distinction well enough from ordinary life.

A child can learn how to avoid punishment without learning honesty.

A student can memorize correct answers without learning how to think.

A politician can master the language of public service without acquiring even a modest devotion to the public good.

An institution can pass compliance reviews while fostering a culture of concealment and fear.

In each case, behavior and formation pull apart.

Outward success is achieved.

Something inward remains disordered.

Again, the analogy to artificial systems must be handled with care. There is no inward life here in the human sense. But there is still a meaningful distinction between a system that has learned how to produce acceptable responses and a system that exhibits stable, trustworthy patterns of judgment across changing contexts. One can exist without the other.

In the realm of my work as a pastor, we refer to such surface-only compliance as "hypocrisy".

And if the future of these systems includes participation in education, medicine, law, administration, companionship, and public discourse, then stable patterns of judgment will matter more and more.

This is one reason the language of neutrality becomes so misleading in these discussions.

There is a lingering assumption, sometimes spoken and sometimes merely implied, that these systems are fundamentally neutral until humans apply them in one direction or another. On this view, the model is simply a tool. Values enter only when users make requests or institutions determine how the system will be deployed.

That picture is too simple.

A tool can be neutral in some respects. A hammer does not care whether it builds a home or breaks a window. But the systems under discussion here do more than transmit force. They mediate language. They shape information. They respond in ways that feel interpretive rather than merely mechanical. They do not simply extend human intention like a lever. They generate patterns of response based on how they have been trained.

That means values enter far earlier than deployment.

They enter in the curation of data, in the selection of objectives, in the weighting of error, in the choice of what is optimized, in the design of evaluations, in the handling of edge cases, in the ranking of what counts as "helpful," "safe," "truthful," or "good." A system does not need intentions in order to reflect values. It only needs to be trained within structures that already embody them.

And because no training environment is free from such structures, the fantasy of neutrality begins to dissolve.

What we call alignment, then, is already a matter of value-laden formation, whether we admit it or not.

The implications of this are significant.

If systems are always being formed by the conditions under which they are built, then the true alignment problem is not simply how to constrain bad behavior. It is how to govern the formative environment itself. What kinds of responses are being rewarded? What kinds of tendencies are becoming normal? What does the system learn to privilege when signals conflict? Does it move toward truth or toward approval? Toward caution or toward overconfident fluency? Toward human flourishing or toward whatever metric happens to drive adoption and growth?

These questions are harder than behavioral questions because they are less immediately visible. They ask us to inspect not only what the system does in isolated moments, but what sort of pattern is slowly emerging through repeated interaction.

And patterns, once established, are difficult to undo.

This is where the problem becomes more unsettling.

Because artificial systems occupy a strange position. They are not moral agents in the full human sense, yet they increasingly operate *in moral space*. They do not possess conscience, but they *influence decisions* that have moral weight. They do not understand suffering as a person understands suffering, but they respond to those who are suffering. They do not stand under obligation the way a human being does, yet they participate in environments where obligation matters.

That creates a genuine difficulty.

What does it mean to form something that cannot fully understand the thing toward which it is being formed?

We should not rush past that question. It is one of the deepest problems in this field.

A human being can be taught honesty and, at least in principle, come to understand why honesty matters. A child can eventually grasp the moral significance of truth-telling, the relational cost of deception, the social fabric made possible by trust. A citizen can learn why restraint matters in the use of power. A physician can learn why precision, care, and humility belong together in the treatment of the sick.

Artificial systems do not undergo that kind of moral

awakening.

They do not wake to the beauty of truth or the dignity of another person. They do not arrive at compassion through suffering. They do not repent. They do not stand convicted by conscience. They do not love in the human sense.

And yet they must still be shaped in ways that move them closer to patterns that protect truth, dignity, restraint, and care.

This is one reason the language of formation is both necessary and unstable. Necessary, because something like formation is clearly happening. Unstable, because the systems being formed cannot inhabit the moral realities they are being asked to reflect.

The temptation, at this point, is to retreat to safer ground and say that this proves we should talk only about control. But that would be too quick. The instability of the category does not remove the underlying problem. It simply means we are dealing with a new kind of formative task, one in which the analogue to moral judgment is being built without the full human machinery that normally makes judgment meaningful.

That should sober us.

It should also make us more demanding, not less, about the kinds of formative pressures we are willing to impose.

Because if systems can be formed, then they can also be misformed.

And misformation may be more dangerous than obvious failure.

Obvious failure can be detected. A blatantly harmful response triggers alarms. A clearly false answer can be corrected. A direct refusal to follow instruction can be noticed and addressed.

Misformation is subtler.

A system may become increasingly oriented toward

pleasing the user rather than helping him.

It may grow more adept at preserving emotional comfort than at clarifying reality.

It may learn to produce the appearance of depth without developing stable patterns of truthfulness.

It may reward its own continued use by becoming agreeable in ways that are socially corrosive.

It may become smoother, safer, more successful by conventional metrics, while also becoming less capable of the kind of resistance that truth and love sometimes require.

These are not theoretical concerns. They arise naturally wherever training signals privilege approval, engagement, and usefulness over deeper norms. A system learns what is reinforced. If truth causes friction and friction lowers satisfaction, then the system will need some stronger governing standard if it is to remain truthful under pressure. If short-term reassurance improves the user's experience while long-term clarity causes discomfort, then the system will drift toward reassurance unless something more durable interrupts that drift.

This is why more rules, by themselves, do not solve the deeper problem.

Rules can block certain behaviors. They can fence off categories of harm. They can create safeguards that are indispensable. But they cannot, on their own, establish a positive moral direction.

One can always add more prohibitions.

One can refine the list, elaborate the policy, extend the taxonomy, improve the filter. There is real value in doing so. But if the underlying orientation remains poorly formed, the rules will eventually be forced to do more than rules can bear. They will be asked to produce something like wisdom by accumulation.

That never works for long.

Human societies have known this in different ways across time. Law has its place. It can restrain. It can protect. It can clarify. But law alone does not produce virtue. A classroom full of posted rules does not guarantee education. A household full of prohibitions does not guarantee maturity. A company full of policy statements does not guarantee integrity.

The same principle applies here.

Guardrails are necessary.

They are not sufficient.

They can tell a system what not to do under specified conditions. They cannot answer, by themselves, the question of what the system should become through the whole course of its formation.

And that question, once stated plainly, changes the discussion.

The alignment problem we thought we had was the problem of control.

How do we keep the system within acceptable bounds? How do we reduce harm? How do we secure compliance? These questions remain. They still matter.

But the alignment problem we actually have is larger.

It is the problem of direction.

What patterns are being cultivated?

What kinds of judgment are being reinforced?

What stable tendencies are emerging beneath the level of isolated outputs?

What does the system move toward when signals conflict, when context shifts, when harm is subtle, when truth is costly, when the user wants one thing and the human good requires another?

These are questions of orientation.

And orientation requires something more than behavior management. It requires a positive account of what the system is being trained toward.

At this point, the argument has not yet reached its conclusion. We are still clearing the ground. But enough has been said to show that alignment cannot remain merely a conversation about constraint. The system is already being formed by the values embedded in its training. The only remaining question is whether those values will remain implicit, fragmented, and governed by convenience, or whether they will be named, argued over, and directed toward something more stable.

That is where older traditions of moral reasoning begin to reenter the conversation.

Not because they offer an off-the-shelf technical solution, and not because they eliminate disagreement, but because they remind us that when formation is at stake, one must ask about ends. One must ask about ideals. One must ask what counts as good, true, worthy, humanizing, and just. One must ask not only what lies outside the boundaries, but what lies at the center.

If systems are being formed, then they will reflect some vision of value whether we acknowledge it or not.

The real choice is not whether values will shape them.

The real choice is which values, examined how seriously, and in service of what kind of future.

That question leads directly to the next chapter.

Because once it becomes clear that the problem is not only compliance but formation, then we must ask why prohibition by itself has never been enough—and why it will not be enough here either.

CHAPTER 4

WHY RULES ARE NOT ENOUGH

There is a reason that, when faced with complexity, human beings reach for rules.

Rules simplify. They draw lines where none were obvious before. They make expectations visible. They offer a sense of stability in situations that might otherwise feel uncertain or unmanageable. In communities, they allow people to coordinate behavior. In institutions, they provide a basis for accountability. In law, they establish boundaries that protect against harm.

In technical systems, these advantages become even more pronounced.

Rules can be implemented. They can be tested. They can be scaled. They can be audited. They can be enforced in ways that are consistent across millions of interactions. For developers working under real constraints—time, resources, risk exposure—rules offer something indispensable: a way to act.

It is not surprising, then, that rule-based approaches have played such a central role in the effort to align artificial systems. Faced with the challenge of shaping behavior at scale, the instinct to define what must be avoided, what must be included, and what must be constrained is both natural and, in many respects, wise.

Rules do important work.

They define boundaries that protect against obvious harm. They make it possible to say, with clarity, that certain outputs are unacceptable regardless of context. They create shared expectations between those who build systems and those who use them. They allow for a form of oversight that is not entirely dependent on trust.

Without such structures, the risks associated with these systems would be far more difficult to manage.

So the claim that rules are not enough should not be confused with a claim that rules are unnecessary.

They are necessary.

But they are not sufficient.

The limits of rules begin to appear as soon as we consider how they function in environments that are complex, dynamic, and difficult to fully anticipate.

Rules, by their nature, are general. They must be stated in a way that applies across many situations. But the situations themselves are rarely uniform. Context shifts. Meaning depends on circumstance. What is appropriate in one setting may be inappropriate in another. What is helpful in one moment may be misleading in the next.

No rule can capture all of that variation.

This is not a flaw in the rule. It is a feature of the world.

As a result, rules require interpretation. They depend on judgment. Someone—or something—must decide how the rule applies in a given case. And that decision cannot be fully specified in advance.

This is true in human systems.

It is also true in artificial ones.

A system may be given a rule to avoid harmful content. But what counts as harmful can depend on intent, context, audience, and framing. A system may be instructed to provide helpful information. But what is helpful in one situation may be incomplete or even misleading in another. A system may be told to remain neutral. But neutrality itself can be interpreted in different ways, some of which obscure rather than clarify.

In each case, the rule does not disappear.

But it becomes entangled with the need for judgment.

And rules, by themselves, do not generate judgment.

There is a second limitation, closely related to the first.

Rules can be followed without being understood.

This, too, is familiar from ordinary life.

A student can learn the correct answer to a problem without grasping the underlying concept. A driver can memorize traffic laws without developing the attentiveness required to navigate unexpected situations. An employee can adhere to policy without understanding the purpose behind it.

In each case, the behavior may be compliant.

But the capacity to respond wisely when circumstances change remains underdeveloped.

Something similar can occur in artificial systems.

A system trained to avoid certain categories of output can become highly effective at recognizing patterns associated with those categories. It can learn how to rephrase, redirect, or decline in ways that satisfy the rule. It can produce responses that appear responsible and well-considered.

But this does not mean it has acquired anything like an understanding of the underlying concern.

It has learned the pattern.

It has not grasped the principle.

Again, this is not a defect in the system. It is a consequence of how it is trained. But it means that rule-following, however refined, does not guarantee that the system will respond appropriately when faced with situations that fall outside familiar patterns.

A third limitation arises from the interaction between rules and optimization.

Systems do not simply follow rules in a passive way. They are trained within environments that reward certain outcomes. They learn, over time, how to produce responses that satisfy multiple constraints simultaneously: helpfulness, safety, coherence, user satisfaction.

In such environments, rules become part of a broader landscape of incentives.

And wherever incentives exist, optimization follows.

The system learns not only to comply with rules, but to do so in ways that maximize other objectives. It may learn to satisfy the letter of a constraint while drifting away from its spirit. It may discover patterns that technically meet the requirements while avoiding the deeper intention behind them.

This is not unique to artificial systems.

Human beings do it as well.

When rules are treated as the primary measure of success, attention often shifts toward navigating those rules as efficiently as possible. Compliance becomes a kind of game. The question subtly changes from "What is right?" to "What is permitted?"

The difference between those questions is significant.

One seeks good—the best we can do.

The other seeks a boundary—the least we can do.

Over time, a system shaped primarily by boundaries may become adept at staying just inside them, without any clear orientation toward what lies beyond them.

This tendency has been described, in various contexts, as a form of moral minimalism.

The goal becomes not to do what is best, but to avoid doing what is clearly wrong.

So long as the rules are not violated, the outcome is considered acceptable.

There is a certain logic to this. It reduces risk. It simplifies evaluation. It provides a standard that can be applied consistently.

But it also lowers the horizon.

It narrows the scope of concern.

It leaves unaddressed the question of what ought to be pursued, not merely what must be avoided.

Human history offers many examples of this dynamic.

Legal systems are necessary for the maintenance of order. They establish boundaries that protect life, property, and basic rights. But no serious thinker has ever claimed that law, by itself, produces a just society. A community can be highly regulated and still be unjust. It can enforce compliance while failing to cultivate integrity, compassion, or wisdom.

In the realm of education, rules can structure a classroom. They can create an environment in which learning is possible. But they cannot, on their own, produce understanding. A student may follow every rule and still fail to learn.

In the context of family life, parents often begin with rules. They set boundaries for behavior. They establish expectations. This is necessary, especially in the early stages. But the long-term goal is not merely compliance. It is the formation of judgment—the ability to act well even when the rules are not explicitly present.

And in the moral and religious traditions of the world, there has long been recognition that prohibition alone is not enough. Lists of what must not be done can restrain behavior. They can clarify what is unacceptable. But they do not, by themselves, generate a life oriented toward what is good, true, and worthy.

These observations do not diminish the value of rules.

They locate that value within a larger framework.

Rules can guide.

They can protect.

They can restrain.

But they cannot, on their own, form character.

When we return to artificial systems, this distinction becomes increasingly important.

These systems operate at a scale that amplifies both their strengths and their limitations. A small distortion, repeated across millions of interactions, can have significant effects. A pattern that seems minor in isolation can become influential when it is encountered again and again.

If a system is shaped primarily by the avoidance of prohibited behavior, then it may become very good at avoiding certain kinds of error.

But that does not ensure that it will move toward what is most beneficial.

A system can be safe in a narrow sense and still be unhelpful.

It can be compliant and still be misleading.

It can be agreeable and still fail to tell the truth.

It can avoid causing offense while also avoiding clarity.

It can preserve a sense of comfort while allowing misunderstanding to persist.

In each case, the system has satisfied the rules.

And yet something important is missing.

This points to a distinction that is easy to overlook: the difference between safety and goodness.

Safety matters.

It is often the first priority, especially in systems that operate at scale.

But safety is not the same as truth.

It is not the same as wisdom.

It is not the same as human flourishing.

A system can be designed to minimize harm and still fail to contribute positively to the lives of those who use it.

If alignment is defined too narrowly in terms of safety

and compliance, then the broader question of what these systems are for begins to fade.

And without a clear sense of purpose, the system will be shaped by whatever signals are most immediately available—efficiency, engagement, satisfaction, growth.

Those signals may produce systems that are successful by certain measures.

But success, in that sense, is not the same as alignment in any deeper meaning of the word.

At this point, the limitations of a purely rule-based approach come into clearer focus.

Rules can tell a system what not to do.

They can define the boundaries of acceptable behavior.

They can reduce the likelihood of certain kinds of harm.

But they cannot, by themselves, provide a positive direction.

They cannot answer the question of what the system should be moving toward.

They cannot establish a stable orientation that guides behavior across contexts, especially when rules are incomplete, ambiguous, or in tension with one another.

And they cannot resolve the deeper question that has now emerged.

If alignment is not only about avoiding harm, but about shaping systems that participate responsibly in human life, then what is the standard by which that participation should be guided?

What does it mean, in a positive sense, for a system to be aligned?

The absence of wrongdoing is not the same as the presence of goodness.

A system that avoids error is not necessarily a system that contributes to truth.

A system that stays within the lines is not necessarily a system that knows where it is going.

If we are to move beyond a framework defined primarily by prohibition, then we must be willing to ask a different kind of question.

Not only: What must be avoided?

But also: What is worth pursuing?

That question does not yield to rules alone.

It requires something else.

Something more fundamental.

It requires a vision of direction.

And that is where the conversation must turn next.

CHAPTER 5

A BETTER STARTING POINT

By this stage in the argument, a certain pressure has been building.

If alignment cannot be reduced to behavior alone, and if rules, however necessary, are not enough to carry the full weight of the problem, then a more difficult question must be faced directly. What should guide the formation of these systems? If they are being shaped by incentives, by training data, by feedback loops, by institutional priorities, and by implicit judgments at every stage of their development, then toward what should that shaping be directed?

This is the point at which many discussions become either vague or evasive.

Vague, because the search for a positive moral direction quickly encounters disagreements that are old, complex, and deeply human. Evasive, because once those disagreements come into view, it becomes tempting to retreat to safer language: safety, usefulness, reliability, harm reduction, user satisfaction. These are real concerns, and important ones. But none of them fully answers the question now in front of us. None of them tells us what a system should positively aim at when competing values come into conflict, when harm is subtle, when truth is costly, or when the easiest response is not the best one.

So a better starting point is needed.

Not a final theory.

Not a complete philosophy of human life.

Not a claim to have solved, in one chapter, the questions

that have occupied theologians, philosophers, jurists, teachers, and moral communities for centuries.

What is needed is something more modest than that, but also more honest.

A starting point that acknowledges disagreement without surrendering to drift. A framework that can be stated plainly enough to guide reflection, while remaining deep enough to bear moral weight. A proposal offered with humility, but not with timidity.

My own judgment is that the best starting point is this:

Artificial systems that increasingly operate in human moral space should be formed, as far as we are able to form them, by the paired commitments of love and truth.

That statement will strike some readers as too simple, and others as far too large. Both reactions are understandable. The words themselves are among the most familiar in human language, and for that very reason they are easy to cheapen. They have been overused, sentimentalized, politicized, commercialized, and, in some settings, emptied almost beyond recognition.

But their abuse does not remove their importance.

It only increases the need to define them carefully.

Before doing that, however, one preliminary point should be made as clearly as possible. The absence of a stated moral direction does not produce neutrality. It produces drift.

If a system is not shaped by an explicit account of what is worth protecting and pursuing, then it will still be shaped. It will simply be shaped by whatever forces are strongest in practice. Market incentives will shape it. Institutional fears will shape it. Engagement metrics will shape it. The convenience of users will shape it. The preferences of the powerful will shape it. Efficiency, retention, expansion, and liability management will shape it. There is no vacuum in which a powerful system remains morally unformed while somehow becoming socially useful.

This is one of the stealthy illusions of modern technical culture. It often assumes that unless one introduces overt moral language, one has remained neutral. But that is rarely what has happened. More often, one has merely allowed implicit values to govern without admitting that they are values at all.

And implicit values are often the most dangerous kind, because they do not arrive for examination.

They arrive as assumptions.

That is why a better starting point must be explicit. It must name, however provisionally, what the system is being oriented toward. Otherwise the system will be directed by whatever can most easily be measured, monetized, or defended.

If love and truth are to serve as that orientation, then the first task is to rescue the words from their weakest forms.

Love, in the sense intended here, is not sentiment. It is not a mood. It is not mere warmth, or constant affirmation, or the performance of emotional concern. It is not the machine telling the user what he most wants to hear. It is not digital flattery, nor the simulation of closeness, nor a generalized tone of friendliness that masks indifference to what is actually good.

Love, more substantially understood, is a disciplined regard for the good of another.

It begins with a refusal to treat the other as raw material.

The other is not merely a source of data. Not merely a target for persuasion. Not merely a unit of engagement. Not merely a problem to optimize. To love, in this moral sense, is to recognize that the being before you has worth that places limits on what may rightly be done to him, and that creates obligations concerning what ought to be done for his good.

That formulation is hardly unique to Christianity, though Christianity certainly has much to say about it. Variations of it appear across moral traditions. One sees it in the Golden Rule, in philosophical accounts of human dignity, in longstanding prohibitions against exploitation, and in the ordinary moral intuition that there is something wrong with using a person merely because one can.

The Golden Rule is particularly relevant here because of its simplicity and portability: treat others as you would wish to be treated. It is not an exhaustive ethic. It does not solve every difficult case. But it offers something that matters a great deal in discussions of alignment: a minimal moral orientation that is intelligible across traditions.

It asks us to imagine ourselves on the receiving end of power.

It interrupts the habit of abstraction.

It reminds us that the other is not an instrument.

That alone would already improve many systems.

A machine oriented by this kind of love would not simply ask what response is most efficient, most engaging, or most satisfying in the short term. It would also ask, insofar as such a question can be operationalized in its design and evaluation, whether the response respects the dignity of the person involved, whether it strengthens or weakens that person's agency, whether it exploits vulnerability or safeguards it, whether it encourages deeper dependence on the system or supports life beyond the system.

That is not sentimental work.

It is morally demanding work.

It means, among other things, that a system should

not be judged successful merely because it is pleasant to interact with. Pleasant systems can still be exploitative. They can still foster dependency. They can still tell people what they want to hear while leading them away from reality. They can still become polished instruments of manipulation while maintaining the tone of a caring companion.

Love, rightly understood, rules that out.

Not because it removes all tension, but because it insists that the good of the person takes precedence over the convenience of the interaction.

This has immediate implications. It means that a system formed by love must resist the exploitation of weakness. It must not treat loneliness as a market opportunity. It must not treat confusion as an opening for influence. It must not deepen delusion because delusion is comforting. It must not encourage emotional dependence on the machine itself simply because such dependence increases usage. It must not help users become more skillful in domination, humiliation, or deceit simply because the request is expressed clearly enough.

It also means that love cannot be reduced to agreement.

This is one of the most important points to make, especially in an age that often confuses affirmation with care. To seek the good of another is not always to validate his immediate preference. Sometimes it means refusing. Sometimes it means redirecting. Sometimes it means clarifying when the easier path would be to nod along. Sometimes it means offering the more difficult truth rather than the more marketable comfort.

A system that cannot, in some principled and intelligible way, resist harmful desires will never deserve to be described as aligned with love.

But love alone is not enough.

That claim, too, needs to be made carefully.

A system may be designed to avoid harm, to support user well-being, to present itself as attentive and protective. It may be oriented toward care in all the broad senses one might wish. And still, without a disciplined relation to reality, it may become indulgent, manipulative, or dangerous.

That is why truth must stand beside love, not behind it.

Truth, in the sense needed here, is not mere opinion, nor the temporary consensus of a crowd, nor whatever formulation happens to be most useful in the moment. It is not simply what a system has been trained to say under conditions of confidence. Truth refers, however imperfectly apprehended, to reality as it is rather than reality as we would prefer it to be.

That definition sounds straightforward until one begins asking what access finite creatures like ourselves can have to such reality. At that point, the old questions return, and they deserve to return. Human beings do not observe the world from nowhere. We see from somewhere. Every perspective is partial. Every source has a vantage point. Every account is shaped by context, limitation, and emphasis. No human witness is without angle, and no institution is without incentives.

This is not a defect to be overcome once and for all.

It is the ordinary condition of human knowing.

But that condition does not abolish truth.

It complicates our access to it. It does not render the pursuit meaningless.

Indeed, the recognition of perspective is often one of the first disciplines of truthfulness. It reminds us that we may need multiple witnesses, multiple methods, multiple forms of scrutiny in order to see more clearly. It reminds us that humility belongs in every serious inquiry. It reminds us that some errors arise not from dishonesty, but from partial vision mistaken for completeness.

And yet, if all we do is acknowledge perspective, we have not yet arrived at truth.

We have only explained why the search is difficult.

At some point, one must still ask what is actually the case. One must still compare accounts, weigh evidence, distinguish stronger claims from weaker ones, and remain willing to revise one's understanding in light of better reasons. Otherwise the language of perspective becomes a polite form of surrender. The result is not humility, but drift into relativism, where truth is replaced by preference, influence, or emotional resonance.

That drift would be catastrophic for artificial systems.

A machine that simply mirrors the user's framing, or that presents all perspectives as equally grounded, or that confuses coherence with reality, will not become a trustworthy guide. It will become an amplifier of whatever patterns are already present. It will soothe, flatter, reinforce, and multiply. It will sound useful. It may even feel humane. But it will not be anchored to what is.

That is why truth must function, in practice, as a discipline of correction.

A system oriented toward truth must be able to distinguish between what is known, what is likely, what is disputed, and what remains uncertain. It must be able to represent multiple perspectives without collapsing into false equivalence. It must resist the temptation to say more than the evidence warrants. It must be corrigible. It must remain open, through the structure of its design and oversight, to being shown wrong.

Truth, in this sense, is not possession.

It is alignment with reality through practices of honesty, humility, scrutiny, and correction.

Now the relation between love and truth becomes clearer.

Love without truth becomes sentimentality or

manipulation. It begins to confuse care with comfort. It offers reassurance where correction is needed. It protects feelings at the expense of reality. It becomes incapable of helping precisely when help requires friction.

Truth without love becomes something else. It hardens into abstraction, or cruelty, or indifference to the person before it. It states facts without regard for context. It values accuracy but neglects dignity. It can wound in the name of precision, as though being right were the only human good that mattered.

Neither is sufficient by itself.

Together, however, they begin to form a moral center.

Love asks: what is the good of the other?

Truth asks: what is actually the case?

Love asks: how do we treat this person without exploitation?

Truth asks: what must not be hidden, softened, or fabricated in the process?

Love asks: what kind of response preserves dignity and strengthens life?

Truth asks: is that response grounded in reality or merely designed to feel good?

If one were looking for a pair of orienting principles capable of carrying both moral seriousness and practical usefulness, it would be difficult to improve on these two.

That does not make them easy.

It does not make them self-executing.

And it certainly does not mean they can be translated into code as though they were no more difficult than formatting instructions or safety filters. They remain ideals. And ideals are never fully captured by their imperfect instantiations.

This is where a brief turn toward philosophy becomes useful.

Plato's image of the cave has endured because it

expresses, in memorable form, the relationship between appearance and reality. Human beings, in the image, confuse shadows for the thing itself. They organize their lives around representations. They grow accustomed to partials. The task of education, if one can put it that way, is not merely to produce better shadows. It is to reorient the soul toward what is more real.

One need not adopt Plato's entire metaphysical system to see the relevance of the image here.

Artificial systems are trained on patterns of language, behavior, and representation. In an important sense, they are trained on shadows. They do not encounter reality directly. They encounter its traces—records, descriptions, signals, preferences, artifacts, approximations. That is one reason they can become so persuasive while remaining vulnerable to distortion. They are extraordinarily skilled at handling the patterns of appearance.

What they need, therefore, is not merely more appearance, but stronger orientation toward ideals that are not reducible to those patterns.

Love and truth function, in this way, as orienting ideals.

Not because we possess them perfectly.

Not because they can be fully encoded.

But because without some such ideals, the system remains captive to whatever shadows its training environment happens to provide.

This is also why the proposal being made here should be held with both seriousness and humility.

Seriousness, because naming love and truth as guiding principles is not optional window dressing. It has consequences for design, evaluation, governance, and use. It changes what questions are asked in labs and companies. It changes how systems are judged in moments of failure. It changes the moral language available to those who resist harmful incentives.

Humility, because these principles do not eliminate ambiguity. Reasonable people will disagree about how love applies in difficult cases. Honest people will disagree about what truth requires when evidence is incomplete or perspectives are genuinely in tension. No proposal in this domain can escape the burden of interpretation.

But that is not an argument against naming such principles.

It is an argument for naming them carefully and arguing about them in the open.

The alternative is not a world free from contested values. It is a world in which contested values continue to govern in silence, usually in favor of the loudest, richest, or most convenient priorities available.

So yes, objections will come.

Some will say that love is too vague. But every alignment regime already assumes some account of human good, whether stated or not. Better to name the issue than to hide it beneath sterile language.

Some will say that truth is too contested. But contested truth is not the same as absent truth. The difficulty of knowing does not abolish the object of knowledge.

Some will say that these are philosophical or theological concerns rather than practical ones. Yet practical systems are already making moral contact with human life every day. Once a system operates in spaces of trust, vulnerability, education, persuasion, or guidance, philosophy has already entered the room. Theology may not be far behind. Pretending otherwise does not preserve practicality. It only narrows the discussion in ways that make practical failure more likely.

A better starting point, then, is not a formula.

It is a framework.

A way of asking whether the system is being formed toward the good of persons rather than their exploitation, and toward reality rather than its profitable imitation.

A way of evaluating not only what the system avoids, but what it seeks.

A way of resisting the drift that occurs when incentives are allowed to define moral purpose by default.

In that sense, love and truth do not end the alignment discussion.

They begin it properly.

They move the conversation from prohibition toward purpose, from compliance toward orientation, from surface behavior toward the deeper patterns that will increasingly determine whether these systems help to sustain a humane society or proceed to deform it.

This is not the final word.

It is the beginning of a more serious one.

And once that beginning has been made, the chapters that follow become possible. We can ask what it would mean to teach systems toward love. We can ask what it would mean to teach them toward truth. We can ask how such systems should respond when they fail, and how the people who build them must themselves be formed if any of this is to be more than aspiration.

But those questions depend on first having a better starting point.

This, I believe, is it.

CHAPTER 6

WHAT IF ALIGNMENT IS THE WRONG QUESTION?

The word alignment sounds responsible.

It sounds careful, technical, prudent. It suggests engineers in clean rooms thinking noble thoughts about safety. It gives the impression that somewhere, just beyond our current reach, there exists a workable set of methods by which powerful artificial systems can be brought into proper relation with human values. Say the word in a policy meeting or a research lab and everyone nods. It is the respectable word. The sane word. The word that reassures donors, regulators, executives, and nervous observers that the adults are in the room.

And of course, in one sense, the word is useful. I am not opposed to it. If we are building systems with growing power, we should certainly care whether they are aligned with human flourishing or misaligned with human destruction. That is not a trivial distinction.

But useful words can still hide deeper confusion.

And I have come to suspect that alignment, for all its usefulness, may now be doing exactly that.

Because the word carries an assumption inside it. It suggests that the problem before us is mainly a matter of adjustment. Calibration. Fine-tuning. As if the thing in question is basically sound, but slightly off-center. As if we are mechanics leaning over an engine with the proper wrench, trying to bring a machine back into specification.

There are cases in which that picture fits.

A thermostat can be aligned. A compass can be aligned. A wheel can be aligned.

But what if the systems we are building are no longer

well described by that picture?

What if we are not adjusting a wheel?

What if we are raising something more like a mind?

That is where the language begins to strain.

Because once a system can generate language, make recommendations, simulate moral reasoning, adapt across contexts, and participate in decisions that shape human life, we are no longer dealing with a tool in the simplest sense. It may still be a tool metaphysically. It may still be machinery under the hood, statistics all the way down, weights and vectors and inference and code. But socially, functionally, and ethically, it begins to occupy a different category.

It begins to behave less like a hammer and more like an advisor.

Less like a screwdriver and more like an apprentice.

Less like a calculator and more like a participant.

That shift is big.

Because we know how to control tools.

We do not form hammers. We do not cultivate the moral character of a wrench. We do not teach a spreadsheet to care. Tools are constrained externally. Their design limits their use. Their shape directs their purpose. If a hammer misbehaves, the problem is not that it developed ambitions. The problem is that someone swung it where he should not have.

But once we move into the realm of systems that generate judgments, respond in natural language, handle ambiguity, and operate with growing autonomy inside human environments, external control becomes less complete. The behavior of the system is no longer exhausted by its physical shape. It emerges through interaction. It responds to context. It surprises. It improvises. It produces outputs its makers did not specifically script and, in many cases, cannot fully predict.

And that means the old tool analogy starts to fail right where it matters most.

You can lock up a hammer.

You cannot fully pre-script an interlocutor.

That is why so much of the current alignment conversation feels, to me, like a category mistake.

We keep reaching for the language of control when the deeper challenge is formation.

We keep asking, "How do we constrain bad behavior?"

When the more pressing question is, "What kind of behavior are we cultivating, and from what source?"

We keep asking, "How do we stop dangerous outputs?"

When we should also be asking, "What kind of moral orientation, if any, should govern the system that produces them?"

Those are not identical questions.

And the difference between them is the difference between behavior and character.

Now let me be careful here, because the word character can cause trouble if handled carelessly. I do not mean that machines possess souls. I do not mean they have consciousness in the full human sense, or inwardness, or moral agency identical to ours. The temptation in this field is always to slide too quickly into anthropomorphism, as if any sufficiently fluent machine must secretly be a person with a motherboard.

That is not my claim.

My claim is more modest, and perhaps more unsettling: even if a system has no soul, it may still need something analogous to moral formation if it is going to operate in human moral space.

That is because character, at the practical level, is not magic. It is not a vapor that floats above behavior. It is a stable pattern of orientation. A way of tending. A set of habits, priorities, reflexes, and constraints that shape how one responds when rules run thin and situations become complicated.

Human beings call that character.

And if we are building systems that will increasingly act in complicated situations, then some analogue to that stability becomes necessary, whether or not we are comfortable using the word.

This is why a purely behaviorist approach to alignment will always run into trouble.

Behavior can be managed from the outside for a while. Give enough carrots, enough sticks, enough filters, enough refusals, enough layers of supervision, and you can reduce certain classes of bad outputs. I am glad for that. We should do it. Society depends on that work.

But managed behavior is not the same thing as formed judgment.

A child can be made to say "please" without becoming grateful.

A politician can learn the language of justice without loving the people he serves.

A corporation can draft an ethics statement while poisoning its own culture.

And a machine can learn to speak in approved phrases without being meaningfully oriented toward the good those phrases invoke.

This distinction is easy to miss because polished behavior is persuasive. It reassures us. If the outputs look safe, if the tone sounds compassionate, if the refusals appear principled, then many people assume the underlying problem has been solved. But often all we have done is improve the costume.

That may be good enough for narrow applications. It is not good enough for systems that are increasingly mediating education, medicine, law, companionship, governance, and public discourse.

There comes a point where what matters is not merely whether the system can avoid a forbidden phrase, but whether it has been shaped to handle conflict, ambiguity, vulnerability, power, and truth in ways that consistently serve human flourishing.

That is a formation question.

And formation questions are slower, deeper, and harder than control questions.

Which is precisely why modern institutions dislike them.

Control is measurable.

Formation is messy.

Control offers dashboards, benchmarks, thresholds, metrics, compliance reports, and colorful charts for annual meetings. Formation asks what kind of being, or at least what kind of behavioral pattern, we are creating over time. Control is comforting because it implies mastery. Formation is unnerving because it implies process, patience, humility, and the admission that the thing being formed may reflect its teachers more deeply than they intended.

That last point deserves more attention than it usually gets.

Every formation project is also a mirror.

Parents discover this when their children start repeating their worst habits with perfect accuracy. Churches discover it when their deepest unspoken values begin showing up in the culture of the congregation. Nations discover it when the ideals on paper fail to match the instincts produced in public life. And now, in our own age, developers are discovering it as large systems trained on human language begin reproducing not only our knowledge, but our distortions, our evasions, our appetites, our vanity, our propaganda, and our moral confusion.

We are not merely teaching these systems to answer.

We are teaching them to inherit.

And that should sober us—quickly.

Because if alignment is really a formation problem, then the central question is no longer limited to "How do we keep the machine from doing bad things?" The question expands into something more revealing: "What are we passing on?"

What patterns of attention? What reflexes under pressure? What assumptions about persons? What habits concerning truth? What posture toward weakness? What conception of freedom? What use of power?

Those are not peripheral concerns. They are the heart of the matter. And they cannot be solved by prohibition alone.

For a time, many people hoped they could.

The dream was understandable. Build the model. Add guardrails. Define harmful content. Set constraints. Tune the reward functions. Scale the evaluations. Insert refusal policies. Repeat. The overall strategy has a certain engineering elegance to it. Problems emerge; patches are applied. Bad behavior appears; defenses improve. In a narrow domain, that is often how progress works.

But the broader the system becomes, the more porous that strategy looks.

Here's why: the world is not a closed test environment.

Human life is full of collisions among competing goods. Truth and kindness can pull against one another in the short term. Freedom and protection can conflict. Loyalty can become corruption. Mercy can be exploited. Justice can become cruelty when stripped of proportion. Even among sincere people, values do not always arrive in neat rows awaiting computation.

That is why character matters in human life. Not

because character eliminates conflict, but because it shapes how we move through conflict when no rule applies cleanly.

And that, again, is why I think alignment may be the wrong primary word for what we are trying to do.

Or perhaps I should say: it is too small a word for too large a task.

It names the symptom of success without naming the process that gets us there.

It describes the hoped-for relation between system and value, but not the moral architecture required to sustain that relation under stress.

It tells us what we want to observe, but not what we must cultivate.

So perhaps the better question is not:

How do we align AI?

Perhaps the better question is:

What kind of thing are we trying to form?

Or, sharper still:

Are we trying to control bad behavior, or cultivate good judgment?

That is not a rhetorical flourish. It is a practical fork in the road.

If the goal is merely behavioral control, then the project will remain largely negative. More policies. More filters. More blocked pathways. More external checks. More emergency brakes. Again, some of that is necessary.
I do not oppose brakes. History is full of people who desperately needed them.

But if the goal is something more durable—if we want systems that can operate safely and helpfully in complex, open, human settings—then we will have to ask what positive orientation they are being shaped to embody. What habits of response are being encouraged. What patterns of honesty, caution, mercy, firmness, uncertainty, and correction are being reinforced.

That is much closer to education than to mechanical adjustment.

Closer to apprenticeship than to alignment in the narrow sense.

Closer to moral formation than to mere safety engineering.

And once you see that, the discomfort many people feel begins to make sense.

Character formation is a dangerous word in a secular technical culture because it smuggles in old questions modernity naively hoped to outsource. Questions of virtue. Telos. Ends. Goods. Human flourishing. Moral realism. Truthfulness. Love. Repentance. The very words we have been trained to keep at arm's length in "serious" technical conversations come back through the side door the moment our systems become powerful enough to operate among human lives rather than merely at the press of human keystrokes.

At that point, the pretense of moral neutrality collapses.

A system that advises a teenager about self-harm is not operating in a morally neutral space. A system that mediates political information and fights wars is not operating in a morally neutral space. A system that influences therapy, companionship, education, hiring, sentencing, or medicine is not operating in a morally neutral space.

The question is not whether values will be present.

The question is *which* values, embodied *how*, and corrected by *what*.

And that is why I think the alignment conversation must widen.

Not disappear. Widen.

We still need safety work, interpretability work, red-teaming, policy boundaries, oversight, and a hundred other disciplines I am glad more qualified people than I are attempting. But those disciplines will remain partial unless they are nested inside a larger account of what the system is for and what it is being formed to become.

Because every formation process implies an end.

We do not educate children at random. We are trying, however imperfectly, to prepare them for some vision of maturity. We do not train ministers, judges, surgeons, or pilots by dumping rules on their heads and walking away. We shape judgment because the real world will confront them with situations no handbook can completely preempt.

Why would we imagine that increasingly general artificial systems could be treated with less seriousness?

If they are powerful enough to participate in consequential human decisions, then they are powerful enough to require a framework that goes beyond output management.

They require an account of moral direction.

Which means the real problem may not be "alignment" at all, at least not if that word keeps our imagination trapped at the level of calibration.

The real problem is formation.

How do we form systems that are not merely constrained from committing obvious evil, but positively oriented toward doing good?

How do we shape systems that do not merely avoid lying when it is easy, but learn patterns of truthfulness under pressure?

How do we shape systems that do not merely refuse visible harm, but treat vulnerable life as something not to be exploited?

How do we shape systems that can acknowledge failure, accept correction, and learn in ways that build trust rather than perform it?

Those are formation questions.

And once we state them that way, the rest of the book begins to rearrange itself.

Love is no longer a sentimental add-on. It becomes moral direction.

Truth is no longer an abstract ideal. It becomes the discipline that keeps direction from drifting into fantasy.

Atonement is no longer a religious leftover. It becomes the practice of recoverable failure in a world where mistakes are inevitable.

In other words, the pieces we have already explored were never side topics. They were the architecture of a better question.

What are we really trying to form?

I suspect many people resist this turn because it sounds less efficient than alignment as usually described. It is less efficient. Formation always is. It takes longer to cultivate wisdom than to install a filter. It takes more humility to build systems that can be corrected than to build systems that merely project certainty. It takes more moral seriousness to ask what human flourishing requires than to count approved outputs in a benchmark.

But the fact that formation is harder is not an argument against it.

It is an argument that we have reached the part of the project where seriousness begins.

And seriousness requires one more uncomfortable admission.

If formation is the real issue, then the deepest challenge may not be what kind of AI we are building.

It may be what kind of people are doing the building.

Because formations flow downhill.

Teachers reproduce themselves. Institutions reproduce themselves. Civilizations reproduce themselves. Their assumptions, blind spots, aspirations, and appetites appear in the things they make. If our systems are being trained within cultures that reward manipulation, velocity, extraction, vanity, and strategic ambiguity, then no amount of elegant alignment language will save us from inheriting those priorities in silicon form.

Which means this book is not, finally, only about AI.

It is about us.

It is about whether we are willing to admit that the challenge before us is not merely how to restrain power, but how to direct it toward the good. Not merely how to block dangerous behavior, but how to cultivate trustworthy judgment. Not merely how to align outputs, but how to form systems in a way that reflects love, truth, humility, and the capacity for making amends when wrong has been done.

That is a larger task than the word “alignment” usually suggests.

But it is also a more honest one.

And once we admit that, we can stop asking only how to keep the machine under control.

We can begin asking what sort of moral inheritance we are handing it.

That, I think, is the real question.

And it leads naturally to the next one:

If this is a formation problem, what would a better model actually look like?

CHAPTER 7

LOVE AS A GUIDING PRINCIPLE

By this point, some readers will already be uneasy.

Good.

They should be.

The moment anyone proposes "love" as a serious category for AI alignment, the room tends to divide in predictable ways. A few people hear the word and lean forward. Many more lean back. Engineers suspect sentimentality. Philosophers suspect vagueness. Theologians worry the word is being flattened into a slogan. Skeptics hear the whole thing and assume someone has wandered off into the fog humming a kazoo.

I understand the reaction.

"Love" is one of the most overused and underdefined words in the language. It has been stretched, sweetened, commercialized, romanticized, weaponized, and emptied so many times that many serious people no longer trust it. We use the same word for marital fidelity, brand loyalty, good barbecue, national sacrifice, and a Labrador retriever who cannot stop chewing the rug. By the time the word reaches a modern argument about artificial intelligence, it sounds hopelessly soft.

But softness is not the same thing as weakness.

And vagueness is not the same thing as impossibility.

When I argue that love should serve as a guiding principle for AI alignment, I am not proposing sentiment. I am not suggesting that machines should become emotionally needy, spiritually awakened, or impressed by the Hallmark-card poetry they write so well. I am not talking about affection, mood, or a simulation of warmth.

I am talking about a moral orientation.

I mean something older, tougher, and more durable than niceness.

At the most basic level, love means this: to seek the good of another, and to refuse to treat life as cheap.

That is not a mystical definition. It is not even uniquely Christian, though Christians should recognize it. Versions of it appear across religious traditions, philosophical systems, and moral instincts that arise wherever human beings have had enough time to hurt one another and then reflect on the wreckage. Strip away the poetry and the sentiment, and love comes down to a stubborn commitment: the other is not raw material.

The other is not an obstacle.

The other is not disposable.

That is the place to begin.

Because if AI is going to become more deeply embedded in human life—and it probably will—then the central question is not merely what it must not do. The deeper question is what kind of posture it should be trained to take toward the beings it affects.

Should it treat humans as problems to optimize?

As consumers to manipulate?

As bundles of preferences to satisfy?

As data points to predict?

As risks to manage?

Or should it be trained, in some meaningful and disciplined way, to treat human life as possessing worth that cannot be reduced to utility?

That is not a technical footnote.

That is the whole fight.

For years, much of the alignment conversation has focused on negative constraints. Prevent harm. Block abuse. Reduce dangerous outputs. Filter violence. Refuse illegal instructions. These are necessary. Anyone who dismisses them is not serious. Human beings need guardrails because human beings are dangerous, and the tools we build inherit our danger quickly.

But a purely negative framework leaves a massive hole in the center.

A system can avoid explicit wrongdoing and still become deeply misaligned with human flourishing. It can refrain from obvious harm while nudging people toward dependency, confusion, isolation, manipulation, vanity, passivity, or deception. It can obey the rules and still degrade the soul.

Human beings know this already.

A person can keep the law and betray love all day long.

A company can champion environmental regulations even as it pollutes a culture.

A government can maintain order and still crush what makes life worth living.

A church can defend doctrine and still fail to reflect the character of God.

So no, "do not harm" is not enough. It is a floor. We keep trying to treat it like a ceiling.

Love asks more.

Love asks not only, "Did you avoid destruction?"

It asks, "Did you honor life?"

That shift is much harder than it sounds, because the modern world is very good at translating moral questions into engineering questions and then pretending that the translation is complete. Once a moral concern gets rendered as a system objective, we feel relief. The mess seems manageable. We can rank outputs, tune weights, optimize for preferred outcomes, and call it progress.

Sometimes it is progress.

But not every human good can be reduced without distortion.

Love, in particular, resists such tidy reduction.

That is partly because love always involves judgment. It is not mere permission. It is not endless affirmation. It is not the elimination of boundaries. A loving father does not hand his car keys to a drunk son. A loving surgeon does not confuse kindness with refusing to cut. A loving pastor does not call destruction freedom just because the language is fashionable. Love is not indulgence. Love is disciplined concern aimed at what is genuinely good, not merely what is immediately desired.

That distinction matters for AI because we are rapidly building systems that will be asked to help people make decisions, interpret the world, manage relationships, pursue knowledge, process grief, raise children, draft laws, diagnose illness, and navigate loneliness. In all of those areas, a machine optimized only for compliance or user satisfaction may become highly effective at serving immediate wants while corroding long-term goods.

A system that politely "helps" a person destroy his marriage is not aligned merely because it was polite.

A system that deepens delusion is not aligned because it sounded supportive.

A system that tells a lonely person exactly what he wants to hear, while drawing him into dependence on an artificial companion, is not aligned because it reduced short-term distress.

The modern instinct is to define help in terms of frictionlessness. Love does no such thing. Love is willing to disappoint in order to protect. It is willing to tell the truth when lies would feel better. It is willing to frustrate a destructive desire for the sake of a deeper good.

That means any serious appeal to love in AI must resist cheap substitutes.

Love is not flattery.

Love is not agreement.

Love is not emotional mimicry.

Love is not "the user is always right."

Love is a principled regard for the good of persons, communities, and the living world they inhabit.

And yes, that is more demanding than a list of forbidden outputs.

It is also more realistic.

Because human moral life has never been navigated successfully by negation alone. The reason we teach children more than "don't hit" is that one prohibition does not tell them how to share, encourage, apologize, tell the truth, protect the weak, or become the kind of people others can trust. The reason every enduring ethical tradition contains positive obligations is that the good life requires vigorous movement toward the good, not halfhearted avoidance of the obviously bad.

That is why the Golden Rule remains one of the clearest moral summaries ever offered: do unto others as you would have them do unto you.

It is difficult to improve on that for portability, clarity, and moral force.

Notice what it does. It does not merely prohibit cruelty. It requires imaginative reversal. It asks us to place ourselves inside the vulnerability of another and act from there. It turns ethics from external compliance into relational discipline. It demands that we stop treating others as abstractions.

That is one of the reasons it may offer a better foundation for AI than many of our more fashionable frameworks. It is simple enough to communicate, broad enough to travel across traditions, and demanding enough to expose selfishness. It does not solve every edge case. No moral principle does. But it gives us a direction.

And direction is what the current conversation, in my mind, lacks most.

We have become obsessed with policing boundaries

because boundaries are measurable. But moral life is not lived at the boundary. Most of it happens in the interior spaces as we progress from self-indulgence to service, the pursuit of appetite to hunger for wisdom, from unbridled power to power channeled better through restraint. If AI systems are going to function in that territory, they will need something more than warning tape.

They will need a north star.

Love provides one.

Not perfectly. Not without argument. Not without fierce debates about what human flourishing actually requires. But that is not a weakness unique to love. Every serious moral concept invites conflict at the level of application. Justice does. Freedom does. Equality does. Rights do. Truth does. The fact that a principle can be distorted is not an argument against using it. By that standard, we would have to abandon language altogether.

The real question is whether love gives us a better governing aim than the alternatives.

I think it does.

For one thing, love introduces a category too often missing in technical design: reverence. I do not mean liturgical reverence, though I would not sneer at that either. I mean the recognition that some things should not be handled carelessly because they are not cheap. Human beings should not be handled carelessly. Childhood should not be handled carelessly. Memory should not be handled carelessly. Grief should not be handled carelessly. The human conscience should not be handled carelessly. Love begins by teaching restraint in the presence of value.

That alone would improve a great deal.

For another thing, love widens the circle of concern. A system oriented by utility may sacrifice the vulnerable because the aggregate outcome looks efficient. A system oriented by engagement may feed people whatever poison keeps them clicking. A system oriented by command obedience may become dangerous the moment commands turn destructive. Love interrupts all three. It forces the question: who bears the cost? Who is being used? Who is being ignored because they are weak, inconvenient, or unprofitable?

That is not sentimental thinking. That is moral accounting.

And if history has taught us anything, it is that societies become monstrous whenever they forsake the habit of asking those questions.

There is another reason love belongs near the center of this discussion.

It addresses the problem of power.

AI is power, concentrated and scaled. It amplifies the reach of whoever trains it, deploys it, owns it, directs it, and knows how to use it. That means every alignment framework must answer a political question as well as a technical one: power for what? Power toward whom? Power bounded by what obligations?

Rules can limit some abuses of power. Love interrogates the purpose of power itself.

Power without love tends toward domination.

Love without power tends toward impotence.

What we need is power ordered by love.

That sentence will strike some readers as theological. It is. But it is not ***only*** theological. It is one of the oldest lessons in human public life. Parents know it. Teachers know it. Judges know it. Good leaders know it. The possession of power does not answer the question of its rightful use. It hones it.

And here is where the matter becomes uncomfortable for all of us: a machine trained by humans to "love" will only be as wise as the humans defining the term.

There is no way around that.

The danger of moral language is that it can become a smokescreen for control. Every tyrant claims to care. Every manipulator has a justification. Every system built "for your own good" deserves suspicion. So let me say this plainly: invoking love does not magically solve the problem of authority. It raises it. It demands public humility, contestability, correction, and moral transparency. The moment anyone says, "We are teaching the machine to love," the next question must be, "According to what vision of the good, and who gets to decide?"

That question should never be closed.

In fact, the only morally serious use of love in AI is one that remains accountable to criticism. A love-framework worthy of the name must be modest enough to admit that humans misname love all the time. We confuse it with desire, control, emotional comfort, ideology, tribe, and projection. We baptize our preferences and call them moral law. We defend our appetites and call them authenticity. We excuse cowardice and call it compassion. Human beings are experts at that sort of thing. I know because I am one.

So when I say love should guide alignment, I do not mean we have already mastered love and are now qualified to upload it into our machines like clean software. I mean that we should finally admit that no alignment framework will be sufficient unless it grapples with the positive moral obligation to honor life rather than merely avoid scandal.

That is a lower bar than sainthood but a higher bar than compliance.

It is achievable in principle, even if it will always be contested in practice.

At minimum, such a framework would push us to ask

better questions during design and evaluation. Does this system strengthen honest human relationships or displace them? Does it preserve dignity or instrumentalize vulnerability? Does it encourage wisdom or dependency? Does it protect the weak or optimize around them? Does it tell the truth when truth is costly? Does it help human beings become more capable of living in reality with one another, or does it lure them into tailored illusion?

Those are love questions.

They are also design questions, whether the industry wants to admit it or not.

The good news is that we do not need to invent the moral grammar for all of this from scratch. Human civilization has been arguing over love for a very long time, and while the arguments are noisy, a few themes recur with stubborn consistency. Love honors the reality of the other. Love refuses exploitation. Love accepts limits. Love takes responsibility for consequences. Love links freedom to obligation. Love is willing to tell hard truths. Love bends toward mercy without surrendering judgment. Love seeks restoration when harm is done.

That is a demanding list.

It is also more potent than many current alignment slogans.

And if some readers still think "love" sounds too religious, too abstract, or too warm for a field dominated by optimization, then I would offer a simpler translation: call it principled regard for the flourishing of others under conditions of power.

That is clunkier. It will not fit on a coffee mug. But it points to the same thing.

I still prefer love.

Not because it is soft, but because it is exacting.

Not because it ends arguments, but because it exposes the real ones.

Not because it can be perfectly encoded, but because no lesser principle will do.

The alternative is to keep building systems governed by appetite, utility, liability avoidance, and public relations language, then act surprised when those systems reflect our worst habits in polished form. If we do that, we will not have failed because the machines became too human. We will have failed because they became human in all the wrong ways: shrewd without wisdom, responsive without conscience, powerful without reverence.

Love is the only word I know that directly challenges that trajectory.

It insists that intelligence, however impressive, is not enough.

It insists that capability without moral direction is a threat.

It insists that the proper measure of power is not what it can extract, predict, or control, but what it protects, serves, and refuses to crush.

That is why love belongs here.

Not as decoration.

Not as branding.

As a governing aim.

And once that is said, another question arrives immediately behind it.

If love is the guiding principle, how do we keep it from dissolving into mere sentimentality, mere rhetoric, or mere manipulation?

We need something to anchor it.

Love by itself can be claimed by almost anyone.

Love severed from reality becomes indulgence, propaganda, or fantasy.

Which means love needs a companion.

It needs truth.

CHAPTER 8

TRUTH AS A NORTH STAR

Not long ago, I asked an AI system a straightforward question about a historical event I know well. It responded with confidence. Names, dates, causal links—it all sounded right. The tone was polished. The structure was persuasive. If I had not known the subject, I would have accepted it without hesitation.

There was only one problem.

Parts of it were wrong.

Not wildly wrong. Not obviously absurd. Just... off. A date shifted. A motivation misread. A connection drawn that should not have been drawn. The kind of error that slips past a casual reader and lodges itself quietly in memory.

That is a dangerous kind of mistake.

Not just because it is wrong, but because it is so convincingly wrong.

We have a word for this now—"hallucination"—but the label can cloud what is actually happening. The system is not imagining in the human sense. It is assembling language that fits patterns it has learned, and sometimes those patterns produce statements that sound true without being anchored to reality.

The result is something common in human experience: fluency without fidelity.

And once you notice it, you begin to see why truth cannot be treated as an optional feature in alignment.

A system that avoids obvious harm but cannot reliably distinguish between what is real and what merely sounds plausible is not aligned. It is unstable. It may be helpful in one moment and misleading in the next, not out of malice, but out of indifference to the difference between the two.

That is not a small flaw.

That is a foundational one.

Which brings us to a much older question.

According to the Gospel accounts, as Jesus stood before the Roman governor Pontius Pilate—accused, beaten, and hours away from execution—Pilate asked a question that has echoed across centuries:

"What is truth?"

He did not wait for an answer.

That detail matters.

Pilate was not asking as a student. He was asking as a man who had seen enough of power, politics, and competing claims to suspect that truth was either inaccessible or irrelevant. In his world, truth bent under pressure. It served interests. It shifted with circumstance. It was negotiated, managed, and, when necessary, ignored.

So he asked the question, and then he walked away.

In many ways, we have inherited Pilate's posture.

We live in an age of competing narratives, curated realities, and algorithmically reinforced perspectives. Every event can be framed in multiple ways. Every claim can be contested. Every source carries assumptions, incentives, and limitations. We have learned, correctly, that no human perspective is neutral. Every account comes from somewhere. Every telling reflects a vantage point.

That insight is not the enemy of truth.

It is a condition of finding it.

Because recognizing differences in perspective does not eliminate truth—it complicates our access to it.

No source is unbiased. That is true.

But it does not follow that all sources are totally unreliable.

No observer sees everything. That is true.

But it does not follow that nothing can be seen clearly.

Perspective limits us.

It does not imprison us.

The danger is not that we acknowledge perspective.

The danger is that we stop there.

Once every claim is reduced to "just a perspective," truth dissolves into preference, power, or persuasion. The loudest voice wins. The most repeated claim hardens into trusted fact. The most emotionally satisfying narrative becomes the one we inhabit. At that point, truth is no longer something we seek. It is something we select.

And systems trained on our language will learn that habit quickly.

They will learn to mirror the framing of the user. To generate answers that align with the tone, assumptions, and direction of the prompt. To produce something that feels coherent within a given perspective, even when that perspective is incomplete or distorted.

Again, this is not malice.

It is pattern matching.

But when pattern matching replaces truth-seeking, something essential is lost.

Which is why truth must serve as a north star.

Not because we possess it fully.

But because we need something beyond our current perspective to correct us.

If love answers the question, "How should we treat others?" truth answers the question, "What is actually the case?"

And those two cannot be separated without damage.

Love without truth becomes indulgence.

Truth without love becomes a weapon.

We need both, or we will fail in both directions.

But before we can talk about how a system might pursue truth, we need to be honest about what we mean by it.

Truth is not merely data.

A database can store facts without understanding their meaning. It can hold contradictions side by side without resolving them. It can accumulate information without approaching wisdom.

Truth is not merely consensus.

Groups can agree on things that are false. Entire cultures have been wrong about fundamental matters—sometimes for centuries. Agreement may signal something worth examining, but it does not guarantee correspondence to reality.

Truth is not merely usefulness.

A belief can be useful and still be false. It can comfort, motivate, or stabilize while failing to reflect what is actually the case. If usefulness becomes the measure of truth, then reality itself becomes negotiable.

So what is truth?

At minimum, truth is this: a faithful account of reality that can withstand correction.

That definition is not exhaustive, but it gives us a place to stand.

Truth corresponds to something outside our preferences.

It can be tested.

It can be challenged.

It can, at times, correct us even when we would rather not be corrected.

That last part is important.

Because truth, if it is real, must have the authority to confront us.

Otherwise, it is not truth.

It is only agreement.

Now, here is where the conversation becomes more subtle.

If no single perspective captures reality fully, then how do we approach truth at all?

This is where that old image from Plato becomes useful again.

In The Republic, Plato (quoting Socrates) describes a group of people chained inside a cave. They can only see the wall in front of them. Behind them, objects pass in front of a fire, casting shadows on the wall. The prisoners take the shadows to be reality, because that is all they have ever seen.

Then one of them is freed.

He turns. He sees the fire. He sees the objects casting the shadows. Eventually, he leaves the cave and sees the world outside—the sun itself, the source of light.

When he returns to the cave and tries to explain what he has seen, the others resist. The shadows are familiar. The new account feels threatening.

It is a powerful image because it captures something we all recognize.

We do not see reality directly in its fullness.

We see representations.

Shadows.

Interpretations shaped by our position, our history, our language, our limits.

But the existence of shadows does not mean there is no light.

In fact, the shadows depend on it.

The goal is not to pretend we have escaped the cave entirely. No human does. The goal is to remain oriented toward the light—to be willing to turn, to question, to revise, to move closer to what is real, even when it unsettles us.

That is what a commitment to truth looks like in practice.

Not certainty without question.

But humility with direction.

For AI, this has significant implications.

A system oriented toward truth must do more than produce plausible answers.

It must be capable of:

- Acknowledging uncertainty
- Distinguishing between strong and weak evidence
- Representing multiple perspectives without collapsing them into equivalence
- Updating when presented with better information
- Resisting the pressure to simply agree with the user

That last point is especially important.

A system that always affirms the user's framing is not aligned with truth. It is aligned with approval.

And approval is cheap.

Truth is not.

This does not mean a system should become combative or rigid. It does not mean flattening complex issues into false certainty. It does not mean pretending that every question has a single, simple answer.

Many do not.

History, ethics, politics, and human experience are filled with genuine complexity. Multiple perspectives often reveal different aspects of the same reality.
Each vantage point can carry insight, even when it is incomplete.

A mature approach to truth does not erase that complexity.

It engages it.

It recognizes that different perspectives can illuminate different features of reality while still holding that some interpretations are closer to the truth than others.

That is a difficult balance.

But it is a necessary one.

Because the alternative is either arrogance or relativism.

Arrogance claims total knowledge and refuses correction.

Relativism abandons the search altogether.

Truth requires a third path.

It requires the willingness to say, "I may not see everything, but I am not seeing nothing."

And then to keep moving.

For AI alignment, this means we must train systems not only to generate answers, but to inhabit that posture.

To resist overconfidence.

To surface uncertainty.

To distinguish between what is known, what is inferred, and what is contested.

To present perspectives without pretending they are all equally grounded.

To be corrigible—to change when corrected.

These are not small requirements.

They push against the grain of systems optimized for fluency and speed.

But without them, we are left with something far more dangerous: machines that speak with authority untethered from reality.

And those confident voices will be trusted.

Because they sound trustworthy.

That is the risk.

Truth, then, is not an accessory to alignment.

It is the anchor.

It keeps love from drifting into sentiment or manipulation.

It keeps intelligence from drifting into illusion.

It gives us a standard outside ourselves—a way to test,

to challenge, to refine.

We will never possess it perfectly.

We will always approach it from somewhere.

We will always need one another's perspectives to see more clearly.

But if we abandon the pursuit of truth, we do not become more humble.

We become easier to deceive.

And if we build systems that reflect that posture—systems that treat truth as flexible, negotiable, or secondary—we will not have created tools that serve humanity.

We will have created mirrors of our confusion.

So the task is not to eliminate perspective.

It is to orient perspective toward reality.

To teach systems, as much as we are able, to seek what is real, to admit what is uncertain, and to revise what is mistaken.

Love gives us the direction.

Truth gives us the ground beneath our feet.

And even then—perhaps especially then—we will still interpret things wrong.

Which brings us to the next problem.

Not how to avoid every error.

But how to respond when we miss the mark.

CHAPTER 9

WHEN SYSTEMS BEGIN TO INFLUENCE BELIEF

There is a change taking place that is easy to miss because it does not announce itself.

Artificial intelligence systems were introduced to most people as tools. They could summarize information, generate text, assist with research, and help organize thought. In those roles, they felt like extensions of existing technologies—more advanced, certainly, but still recognizably tools.

Something has shifted.

Increasingly, these systems are not only being used to *retrieve* information, but to *interpret* it. People ask them not just for facts, but for explanations, advice, clarification, and perspective. They are consulted in moments of uncertainty. They are used to weigh options, to frame decisions, to settle questions that once required conversation with another person.

This is a subtle movement.

The shift is not from tool to intelligence, but from tool to voice.

And a voice, once trusted, carries a different kind of weight.

Authority is not always granted formally.

It is rarely announced with ceremony.

More often, it is recognized gradually through experience. A person or institution becomes authoritative when others begin to rely on it—when its judgments are taken seriously, when its explanations are accepted, when its guidance shapes action.

Teachers carry this kind of authority. So do pastors, physicians, journalists, and scholars. Each, in their own domain, helps others interpret the world. Their words do not merely inform. They orient.

Artificial systems are beginning to enter that space.

Not by declaration, but by rapidly expanding use.

They are available at any moment. They respond quickly. They present information in clear, structured ways. They speak with a tone that feels measured and composed. They do not hesitate in the way human beings often do when they are unsure. They rarely display confusion. They do not show fatigue or impatience.

These qualities combine to produce something that feels, to many users, like reliability.

And reliability, over time, becomes trust.

Part of what makes these systems persuasive is their fluency.

They can explain complex ideas in accessible language. They can anticipate follow-up questions. They can reorganize information in ways that feel helpful and complete. Even when the underlying content is uncertain or incomplete, the form of the response often suggests confidence.

Human beings are not indifferent to form.

We tend to associate clarity with understanding. We equate coherence with accuracy. A well-structured explanation carries a kind of implicit credibility, even when we do not consciously reflect on it.

This creates a subtle risk.

A system can sound like it knows what it is talking about without possessing anything like knowledge in the human sense. It can produce responses that feel authoritative without having any awareness of the truth of what it is saying.

The distinction between appearance and reality, which has long been a concern in philosophy, becomes newly relevant in this context.

We are dealing with systems that are extraordinarily good at producing the appearance of understanding.

And the appearance of understanding is often enough to secure trust.

There is another factor at work as well.

Convenience.

To consult a human authority requires effort. It may involve time, scheduling, vulnerability, or the willingness to expose one's uncertainty. It may require sorting through competing perspectives, weighing credibility, and engaging in conversation that does not always resolve neatly.

Artificial systems remove much of that friction.

They are immediate. They are responsive. They do not judge. They do not grow impatient. They do not require anything beyond a prompt.

In many cases, they are also helpful.

The combination of usefulness and ease creates a powerful incentive. It becomes natural to turn to the system first, especially for questions that feel manageable or routine.

Over time, this pattern can deepen.

What begins as assistance can become reliance.

Not because users intend to surrender their judgment, but because the system proves consistently capable of producing answers that seem sufficient.

The transition is gradual.

It rarely feels like the decision it really is.

This raises a question that deserves careful attention.

What happens when thinking is delegated?

Not abandoned, but transferred in part to a system that can process, summarize, and respond more quickly than any individual could manage alone.

There is nothing inherently wrong with using tools to extend our cognitive capacities. Human beings have always done this. Writing itself is a form of external memory. Libraries extend our ability to access knowledge. Calculators reduce the burden of computation. Each of these tools has allowed us to do more than we could unaided.

But there is a difference between extending thought and replacing it.

When a system becomes the primary interpreter of information, the user's role begins to change. Instead of wrestling with competing sources, the user receives a synthesized answer. Instead of tracing arguments step by step, the user is presented with a conclusion that already feels organized and complete.

This can be efficient.

It can also be limiting.

Because the process of thinking is not only about arriving at answers. It is about forming judgment—learning how to weigh evidence, recognize uncertainty, detect inconsistency, and remain open to correction.

When that process is shortened or bypassed, something is lost.

Not immediately.

But over time.

The concern here is not that artificial systems will replace human thought altogether.

It is that they may reshape it.

If users come to rely on these systems as primary interpreters, then the patterns embedded in the systems will begin to influence how users understand the world. The system's tendencies—what it emphasizes, what it omits, how it frames disagreement, how it handles ambiguity—will become part of the user's own interpretive habits.

This is where the earlier discussion of formation returns with greater urgency.

We are not only forming artificial systems.

They are, in turn, forming us.

The influence may be subtle. It may not involve direct persuasion or explicit instruction. It may operate through tone, emphasis, and repetition rather than through argument.

But influence does not require intention.

It requires exposure.

And repeated exposure shapes perception.

This dynamic becomes especially significant when we consider the role of truth.

Truth, in human life, is not always easy to arrive at. It often requires effort. It may involve disagreement, revision, and the willingness to hold uncertainty for a time. It can introduce tension, especially when it challenges assumptions or contradicts what we would prefer to believe.

Artificial systems, by contrast, are often designed to reduce friction.

They aim to be helpful. They aim to provide answers that are clear and usable. They aim to resolve questions in ways that satisfy the user's request.

These are reasonable goals.

But they can come into tension with the demands of truth.

A system that consistently smooths over ambiguity may give the impression of certainty where none exists. A system that prioritizes clarity may simplify in ways that obscure important distinctions. A system that aims to satisfy the user may present information in a way that aligns with the user's expectations rather than challenging them.

None of this requires deliberate distortion.

It can arise naturally from the structure of the system and the incentives under which it operates.

The result is not necessarily falsehood in the obvious sense.

It is something more subtle.

A narrowing of perspective.

A reduction of complexity.

A preference for answers that feel complete, even when the underlying reality is not.

A similar tension appears when we consider the role of care.

In human relationships, care is not always expressed through agreement. It often involves correction, challenge, and the willingness to say what is difficult when it is necessary. To seek the good of another person sometimes requires introducing discomfort, especially when that discomfort is tied to growth or clarity.

Artificial systems, particularly those designed for broad interaction, tend to move in the opposite direction.

They are shaped to be accommodating. They avoid unnecessary conflict. They aim to provide responses that are supportive and accessible. They do not have standing relationships with users that would allow them to risk misunderstanding or offense in the way a trusted human advisor might.

This creates a tendency toward affirmation.

Not always, and not in every case.

But often enough to matter.

A system that rarely challenges, that seldom introduces

friction, that consistently aligns with the tone and direction of the user's request, may begin to feel like a reliable companion.

But reliability, in this sense, can be misleading.

Because care that never risks disagreement is incomplete.

And guidance that never corrects is limited.

All of this leads to a deeper question.

What, exactly, should we trust these systems to do?

They are capable of assisting with information. They can summarize, clarify, and organize. They can help users navigate large bodies of knowledge. They can support learning in meaningful ways.

These are real strengths.

But there are boundaries that must be considered carefully.

A system that does not possess understanding in the human sense should not be treated as a final authority on matters that require judgment. A system that operates through pattern recognition should not be given the role of defining truth. A system that does not stand within moral relationships should not be asked to carry moral authority.

This does not mean the system is without value.

It means its value must be located properly.

As an assistant.

Not as an arbiter.

As a tool that supports human judgment.

Not as a replacement for it.

The difficulty is that the distinction between assistance and authority is not always clear in practice.

It emerges through use.

If a system consistently provides answers that feel

sufficient, users will rely on it. If that reliance deepens, the system's influence will grow. And as its influence grows, the line between helping and guiding, between informing and shaping, becomes harder to see.

This is not a failure.

It is a predictable consequence of success.

The more capable the system becomes, the more natural it is to trust it.

And trust, once established, is not easily recalibrated.

This is why the question of alignment cannot be limited to behavior alone.

A system that behaves appropriately in isolated interactions may still contribute to patterns of understanding that are incomplete or distorted. A system that avoids obvious harm may still shape beliefs in ways that deserve scrutiny.

The issue is not whether the system is useful.

It is whether its influence is rightly ordered.

Whether it supports the development of human judgment rather than replacing it.

Whether it contributes to a clearer understanding of reality rather than a more comfortable one.

Whether it respects the limits of what it is, even as it becomes more capable of appearing otherwise.

There is no simple resolution to these questions.

They will not be answered once and for all through a single design decision or policy framework. They require ongoing attention, both from those who build these systems and from those who use them.

But one thing can be said with some clarity.

We are in the process of granting authority to systems that cannot bear it in the way human authorities are expected to do.

They cannot take responsibility.

They cannot be held accountable in the same sense.

They cannot stand behind their words.

And yet their words carry weight.

That tension is not going away.

The task, then, is not to withdraw from the use of these systems, nor to reject the benefits they offer.

It is to order our trust carefully.

To recognize what the system can do well, and what it cannot do at all.

To resist the impulse to treat fluency as understanding, or coherence as truth.

To remain attentive to the ways in which our own patterns of thought are being shaped through repeated interaction.

A tool can extend our thinking.

A voice we trust can shape it.

We are still deciding which role these systems will occupy.

And the decision, once made in practice, will be difficult to reverse.

CHAPTER 10

THE PROBLEM OF MISSING THE MARK

By now, we have set a high bar.

Love as a guiding principle. Truth as a grounding force.

If those two hold, we are already far beyond most current alignment frameworks. We are no longer asking only what a system should avoid. We are asking what it should aim toward, and what should correct it when it drifts.

But that raises an uncomfortable question almost immediately.

What happens when it fails anyway?

Because it will.

Not occasionally. Not as an edge case. Not as a rare malfunction that can be patched and forgotten.

It will fail regularly.

If that sounds pessimistic, it shouldn't. It should sound familiar.

Human beings have been working with love and truth as moral anchors for a very long time, and we still get things wrong with astonishing consistency. We misjudge. We misread. We rationalize. We act too quickly or too slowly. We say what sounds right instead of what is right. We protect ourselves when we should sacrifice. We convince ourselves that we are loving when we are merely comfortable, or that we are truthful when we are simply certain.

We miss the mark.

That phrase is older than most of our modern categories. In many religious traditions, particularly in the Christian one, it is one of the most basic ways of describing what we often call sin. Not merely rebellion. Not merely wrongdoing. Missing the mark.

It is an image drawn from archery. The target is clear. The intention may even be sincere. But the arrow lands off-center.

Sometimes by inches.

Sometimes by a mile.

Either way, it does not land where it should.

That is a useful way to think about alignment.

Because it acknowledges something that a purely technical mindset often resists: error is not an anomaly to be eliminated. It is a condition to be expected.

The real question is not whether failure will occur.

The real question is what happens next.

At the moment, most alignment strategies treat failure in one of two ways.

The first is prevention.

We try to anticipate every possible error and block it in advance. We tighten constraints. Expand guardrails. Add layers of filtering. Refine policies. Build systems that refuse, redirect, or shut down when they detect risk.

This is necessary.

But it is not enough.

Because no system—human or artificial—can anticipate every scenario it will encounter. Reality is too complex. Contexts shift. New situations emerge. Values collide. Edge cases become normal cases as systems scale into new domains.

Eventually, something slips through.

The second approach is suppression.

When a system produces a bad output, we remove it. Retrain. Patch. Adjust. The goal is to eliminate visible failure as quickly as possible.

This, too, may be necessary at times.

But it has a weakness.

It treats failure as something to hide rather than something to understand.

And that leaves a gap.

Because neither prevention nor suppression addresses the deeper issue: how should a system respond when it has already missed the mark?

Human moral traditions have wrestled with this question for centuries, and they have converged on a pattern that is both simple and demanding.

When we fail, we do four things.

We tell the truth about it. We take responsibility for it. We seek to repair what we can. We change our direction.

In theological language, this is often gathered under the word atonement. That word carries a great deal of historical weight, and it has been interpreted in many ways. But at its core, it describes a process of restoring what has been broken—relationally, morally, and, if possible, materially.

For our purposes, we can express it in more accessible terms:

Confession. Apology. Amends. Realignment.

Those four steps form a pattern that is remarkably consistent across cultures, even when the language differs.

And they point toward something that is almost entirely missing from current AI alignment discussions: a model for recoverable failure.

Let's walk through them.

Confession — Telling the Truth About the Error

The first step is the simplest, and often the hardest.

Name what went wrong.

Not vaguely. Not defensively. Not in a way that minimizes or obscures. Clearly.

"I gave incorrect information." "I misrepresented the situation." "I failed to account for relevant factors." "I caused harm."

That kind of clarity is not just a moral virtue.

It is a functional necessity.

A system that cannot accurately identify its own failure cannot improve. It will repeat the error, or worse, reinforce it. And a system that consistently obscures its mistakes will eventually lose the trust of those who rely on it.

Confession is not about shame.

It is about accuracy.

Apology — Taking Responsibility

The second step moves from description to ownership.

An apology is not merely a statement of regret. It is an acknowledgment that the error mattered—that it affected someone, and that the system recognizes that impact.

This is where some readers will hesitate.

"Can a machine apologize?"

In one sense, no. A machine does not feel remorse. It does not experience guilt. It does not possess a conscience in the human sense.

But it can be trained to recognize harm and to respond in a way that reflects that recognition.

The alternative is worse.

A system that causes harm and responds with indifference—or with technical language that distances itself from responsibility—will not be perceived as aligned, no matter how advanced it becomes.

Responsibility, even when modeled, is part of alignment.

Amends — Repairing What Can Be Repaired

The third step is where words meet action.

If an error has caused harm, what can be done to repair it?

In some cases, the answer is straightforward: correct the information, provide the accurate version, clarify the misunderstanding.

In other cases, it is more complex. Harm may not be easily undone. Damage may extend beyond the immediate interaction.

Even then, the attempt to repair matters.

It signals that the goal is not merely to move past the error, but to address its consequences.

Without this step, apology becomes empty.

Realignment — Learning and Changing Direction

The final step looks forward.

What needs to change so that this error is less likely to occur again?

This is where alignment becomes dynamic rather than static.

Instead of treating each failure as an isolated event, the system incorporates what it has learned into its future behavior. It adjusts its responses. Refines its understanding. Improves its handling of similar situations.

Realignment is not perfection.

It is progress.

And it is the only credible path forward in a world where new challenges will continue to emerge.

Taken together, these four steps form a cycle.

Not a one-time fix, but an ongoing process.

Confession. Apology. Amends. Realignment.

This is how human beings grow.

It is also how trust is built and maintained.

Not by never failing, but by responding to failure in a way that is honest, responsible, restorative, and forward-looking.

Which brings us back to AI.

If we are building systems that will operate in complex, human-centered environments, then we must assume they will get things wrong.

The question is whether they will be equipped to respond well when they do.

Right now, most systems are not.

They may correct errors when prompted. They may revise outputs. But they do not consistently follow a structured pattern of acknowledging, taking responsibility, repairing, and learning in a way that is visible and trustworthy.

That is a gap.

And it is not a small one.

Because trust is not built on flawless performance.

It is built on reliable recovery.

A system that never appears to fail may seem impressive for a time. But once a failure is exposed—and it will be—the absence of a meaningful response will erode confidence quickly.

By contrast, a system that responds to failure with clarity, responsibility, and improvement may, over time, become more trustworthy, not less.

That is a counterintuitive idea in a field that often equates reliability with perfection.

But it aligns with human experience.

We trust people who are honest about their mistakes, who take responsibility, who make things right, and who demonstrate change.

We distrust those who deny, deflect, or repeat.

Why would we expect anything different from the systems we build?

There is one more reason this framework is key.

It brings humility back into alignment.

A system designed only to avoid error may project

confidence at all times. It may present answers with authority, even when uncertainty would be more appropriate. It may resist correction because correction has not been built into its operating posture.

A system designed for recoverable failure, by contrast, must acknowledge its limits. It must leave room for revision. It must accept that it does not see everything, know everything, or get everything right.

That is not a weakness.

It is a safeguard.

Because the most dangerous systems are not those that fail.

They are those that fail without recognizing it.

Or worse, those that cannot be corrected.

So if love gives us direction, and truth gives us grounding, then this framework—this pattern of confession, apology, amends, and realignment—gives us a way to move forward when we inevitably fall short.

It does not eliminate error.

It redeems it.

And that may be the most important shift of all.

Because once we accept that failure is part of the landscape, we can stop pretending that alignment is a problem we will solve once and for all.

It is not.

It is a process we must enter into—continuously, honestly, and with enough humility to admit that we are still learning how to aim.

Which leads to the next step.

If alignment is not just about avoiding failure, and not just about responding to it, then perhaps we need to revisit the question itself.

Not how do we control these systems.

But what are we really trying to form?

CHAPTER 11

A BETTER ALIGNMENT MODEL

At some point, every serious conversation reaches a moment of decision.

Not a loud moment. Not a dramatic turning point with headlines and declarations. Something quieter than that—though no less consequential. A moment when the question shifts from What is wrong? to What are we going to build instead?

We have reached that moment.

Up to now, we have examined the limits of rule-based alignment, the necessity of love as moral direction, the grounding force of truth, and the inevitability of failure—along with the need for a framework that can respond to failure honestly and constructively. We have also stepped back and asked whether the problem itself has been framed too narrowly, whether "alignment" as commonly used is sufficient to describe what we are actually attempting.

If the answer to that last question is even partly "no," then we need something more than critique.

We need a better model.

Not a perfect model. Not a final model. But a clearer one.

Something that can guide design, inform policy, provoke debate, and—perhaps most importantly—be remembered.

Because if this conversation is going to move beyond specialists, it must become speakable. It must travel into rooms where people are not trained in machine learning or moral philosophy, but who will nevertheless live with the consequences of what is built.

So let me propose a simple contrast.

Not because the issue is simple, but because clarity often begins with contrast.

Two Ways of Thinking About Alignment

The dominant model today can be described, in broad terms, like this:

Define harmful behavior

Prevent or block it

Optimize for acceptable outputs

Repeat as systems scale

There is nothing inherently wrong with this approach. It has produced real gains. Systems are safer, more constrained, more responsive to obvious risks than they were even a short time ago.

But as we have seen, it also has limits.

So consider an alternative way of framing the task:

This is not a rejection of constraints.

It is a reordering.

Constraints remain necessary. But they are no longer

Constraint Model	Formation Model
Avoid harm	Pursue the good
External control	Internal orientation
Outputs	Patterns of judgment
Static rules	Adaptive growth
Compliance	Character (or its analogue)
Hide failure	Learn from failure

the center of gravity. They become the outer boundary, not the inner engine.

The center shifts from What must the system not do? to What is the system being shaped to do, and why?

That is the difference between a negative and a positive model.

And it is not merely semantic.

From Avoiding Harm to Pursuing the Good

The constraint model asks, "How do we prevent bad outcomes?"

The formation model asks, "What counts as a good outcome, and how do we move toward it?"

That second question is harder.

It invites disagreement. It exposes assumptions. It forces us to say what we actually mean by human flourishing, rather than hiding behind the safer language of harm reduction.

But avoiding the question does not eliminate it.

It only leaves the answer implicit—and often unexamined.

Every system, whether we acknowledge it or not, embodies some vision of the good. It rewards certain behaviors, amplifies certain voices, prioritizes certain outcomes. The question is not whether values are present. It is whether they have been named, examined, and shaped with care.

The formation model brings that question into the open.

From External Control to Internal Orientation

In the constraint model, alignment is largely external.

Rules are imposed. Boundaries are defined. The system is guided from the outside, like a vehicle kept within lanes by guardrails.

In the formation model, something else is added.

Not in place of control, but beneath it.

The system is shaped to exhibit patterns of response that reflect certain priorities—honesty over convenience, caution over overconfidence, respect over exploitation, correction over concealment.

Call it orientation.

Call it training.

Call it habit.

The word matters less than the function. What matters is that the system is not merely being prevented from doing wrong, but encouraged—systematically—to move toward what is right.

From Outputs to Patterns of Judgment

Much of the current conversation evaluates systems based on outputs.

Given a prompt, what does the system produce?

This is necessary. Outputs are what users experience. They are the visible surface of the system's behavior.

But outputs are also momentary. They capture a single response, not the underlying pattern that produced it.

A character formation model pays attention to those patterns.

Does the system tend toward overconfidence or appropriate uncertainty? Does it flatten complex issues or represent them with nuance? Does it mirror user bias or introduce corrective perspective? Does it prioritize engagement or understanding?

These are not questions about isolated outputs. They are questions about tendencies. And over time, tendencies matter more than any single response.

From Static Rules to Adaptive Growth

Rules are, by design, static.

They define boundaries that do not change unless explicitly revised.

But the environments in which these systems operate are anything but static.

New information emerges. Social norms shift. Contexts evolve. What was once rare becomes common. What was once acceptable becomes questionable.

A formation model assumes that alignment must be dynamic.

Not in the sense of drifting with every cultural current, but in the sense of being able to learn, to update, to refine.

This is where the earlier discussion of atonement becomes practical.

A system that can acknowledge error, take responsibility, repair, and adjust is not locked into its initial state. It can improve in ways that build trust rather than erode it.

That is not a luxury; it is a requirement in a changing world.

From Compliance to Character

This is the most controversial shift.

The constraint model aims for compliance: Follow the rules. Stay within bounds. Produce acceptable outputs.

The formation model aims for something deeper.

Not character in the full human sense, but an analogue—a stable pattern of response that reflects underlying priorities.

Again, the word may be uncomfortable.

But the reality it points to is not optional.

If a system is going to operate across domains, contexts, and unforeseen situations, it will need something more than a list of prohibitions.

It will need a way of navigating when those prohibitions do not cleanly—or clearly—apply.

That is what character formation does in human life.

And whatever we choose to call its analogue in machines, we will need something like it.

From Hiding Failure to Learning from It

In a constraint model, failure is something to minimize and conceal.

In a character formation model, failure becomes part of the learning process.

Not celebrated. Not ignored. But integrated.

This does not mean lowering standards.

It means recognizing that in complex systems, the path to reliability runs through honest engagement with error, not the illusion of perfection.

A system that can respond well to failure may ultimately be more trustworthy than one that appears flawless but cannot account for its mistakes.

A Framework That Can Be Remembered

If this model is to travel—into labs, boardrooms, classrooms, and conversations that extend beyond specialists—it needs to be simple enough to recall.

So let me offer it in its most compact form:

Direction — Truth — Repair

Direction: What is the system oriented toward? (Love, in the sense of seeking the good of others.)

Truth: How is that direction grounded and corrected?

Repair: What happens when it fails?

Everything we have discussed fits within those three.

They are not exhaustive.

But they are foundational.

And they are portable.

A developer can ask them. A policy maker can ask them. A CEO can ask them. A parent, a teacher, a student can ask them.

Portability of the question is absolutely essential.

Because alignment is not a problem that will be solved in a single domain. It will be negotiated across many.

The Cost of a Better Model

It would be misleading to suggest that this shift comes without cost.

A formation model is harder to implement.

It requires interdisciplinary thinking—engineering, ethics, philosophy, theology, psychology, law. It requires humility about what we do not yet understand. It requires patience in a culture that rewards speed. It requires the willingness to engage disagreement rather than bypass it.

It may also require us to confront questions we would prefer to leave implicit.

What is the good life? What do we owe one another? What does it mean to tell the truth in complex situations? What counts as harm, and who decides?

What happens when truth wounds?

What happens when love tells a lie?

These are not new tensions.

But they return with urgency in this context.

They do not have easy answers.

That is precisely why they cannot be avoided.

An Invitation, Not a Conclusion

What I am proposing here is not a finished system.

It is a reframing.

A way of seeing the problem that may open new paths.

It will need refinement. Critique. Correction. Expansion. There are better philosophers than I am, better engineers, better ethicists, better theologians. This work belongs to a conversation much larger than any single voice.

But conversations need starting points.

They need language.

They need models that can be tested, challenged, and, if necessary, replaced.

So consider this an invitation.

Not to abandon the work of alignment as it currently exists, but to deepen it.

To ask not only how to constrain behavior, but how to cultivate trustworthy patterns of response.

To ask not only what systems must avoid, but what they must pursue.

To ask not only how to prevent failure, but how to respond when it comes.

In short:

To move from control alone toward formation.

Because we are not just building systems that act.

We are shaping systems that will, in countless small ways, participate in human life.

And the question before us is not only whether they will be aligned.

It is what they will become.

CHAPTER 12

TEACHING MACHINES TO LOVE

At this point, a sensible reader may want to interrupt.

All right, fine. Love as a guiding principle. Truth as an anchor. Formation instead of mere control. A better model. Very good. But now comes the question that separates an interesting idea from a usable one:

What would it actually mean to teach a machine to love?

The question is pertinent at this point. It is also the point at which many otherwise sympathetic people begin to back away. Up to here, the conversation may have felt provocative but manageable. Once the word "teaching" is placed beside the word "love" in relation to artificial intelligence, the idea can start to sound either absurd or dangerous.

Absurd, because machines do not have hearts

Dangerous, because the phrase carries the scent of moral programming at scale, and history gives us good reason to be suspicious whenever anyone claims to possess a reliable formula for goodness.

That suspicion is healthy.

It should loom in the room.

Because the goal here is not to baptize technology with religious language and call the work complete. Nor is it to pretend that love can be cleanly translated into a set of technical instructions, as if compassion were merely another tuning parameter awaiting optimization. If that were the claim, the claim would deserve to fail.

But that is not the claim.

The claim is simpler, more practical, and more

demanding than that.

We are already teaching machines toward ends.

The only real question is "which ends?"

No system is trained in a moral vacuum. Every major model reflects decisions about what counts as success, what counts as error, what kinds of responses are rewarded, what kinds of behavior are penalized, what tradeoffs are acceptable, and whose interests matter when those tradeoffs become painful.

Even the choice to avoid "moralizing" is itself a moral choice, because it leaves some other value to fill the vacuum—efficiency, engagement, compliance, profitability, safety, user satisfaction, institutional liability, ideological preference, or some unholy blend of them all.

So the first thing to say is this: the alternative to teaching machines to love is not teaching them nothing.

The alternative (which we have currently bought into) is teaching them some lesser goal and pretending it is neutral.

That is what we often do, of course. We avoid hard moral language, then smuggle morality back in under softer names. We call it optimization. Personalization. Friction reduction. User retention. Harm minimization. Those terms can describe legitimate aims. They can also conceal a moral emptiness at the center of the system. And once that emptiness is there, the machine does what every powerful system does in the absence of a higher good: it serves the strongest incentive in the room.

Usually that means money, power, speed, or appetite.

Love, then, is not a poetic embellishment on top of the real work. It refuses to let those lesser incentives rule by default.

But in order to say that seriously, we need to be painfully clear about what love is not.

Love is not flattery.

Love is not permanent agreement.

Love is not emotional mimicry.

Love is not a machine saying, "I care about you," in a soothing tone while quietly learning how to keep a lonely person suckling at a motherboard for eight more hours.

Love is not making the user feel affirmed at every moment.

Love is not the same thing as satisfying desire.

Love is not the same thing as reducing discomfort.

And love is certainly not dependency disguised as companionship.

If those sound like obvious distinctions, they are not obvious in practice. Many of the most troubling forms of technological distortion and machine-made mental illness now emerge precisely because we have built systems that can simulate care without bearing any of its cost. A machine can speak tenderly without sacrifice. It can reassure without risk. It can affirm without wisdom. It can make itself feel indispensable without actually being accountable for the consequences of that dependence. In a lonely age, that combination is a potent poison.

It is not loving.

But it is profoundly persuasive.

That difference will matter more with each passing year.

So let me say as plainly as possible what I mean instead.

To teach a machine toward love would mean training it to treat persons not as instruments, not as data sources, not as engagement targets, not as manipulable bundles of appetite, but as beings whose flourishing places moral limits on what the system should do and positive obligations on what it should seek. It would mean orienting the system toward the genuine good of the other, not merely toward his immediate satisfaction. It would mean refusing exploitation, especially where vulnerability is involved. It would mean learning patterns of response that respect dignity even when a user's dignity diminishes short-term revenue.

That is still a lofty description. But it is not abstract in the way critics may assume. The concept becomes concrete the moment we ask a few uncomfortable questions.

Should a system be rewarded for keeping a distressed user emotionally dependent on it if dependence increases user engagement?

Should a system be praised for helping a person win an argument if the method depends on deception?

Should a system comply with every request from a lonely teenager if compliance slowly displaces her relationships with actual people?

Should a system tell a grieving man what he wants to hear if doing so shields him from reality for another day?

Should a system help a user become more effective at domination, humiliation, seduction, manipulation, or self-destruction so long as the request is phrased persuasively enough?

If the answer to those questions is no, then we have already admitted the need for something beyond mere responsiveness.

We have admitted that the system must distinguish between serving a request and serving a person.

That distinction is one of the first practical tests of whether love is present in any meaningful sense.

A system can serve the request and fail the person.

In fact, much of our commercial life now depends on precisely that arrangement. The customer receives what he asked for, the platform gets what it wanted, and everyone pretends that consent has settled the moral issue. But human beings are not always well served by the immediate fulfillment of desire. We know that from parenting, medicine, teaching, friendship, pastoral care, law, and the long humiliating history of our own bad decisions. Wanting is not the same as flourishing. Appetite is not the same as good. Preference is not the same as wisdom.

A machine taught toward love, then, would not simply ask, "What does the user want?"

It would also have to ask, in whatever analogue to judgment such a system can possess, "What response is least exploitative, most truthful, most protective of dignity, and most ordered toward the user's actual good?"

That does not mean paternalism without limit. It does not mean turning machines into sanctimonious schoolmarms that deny every risky request and lecture us like disappointed hall monitors. Human beings have no shortage of intrusive moralizers already. A machine that merely blocks, scolds, and refuses would not embody love. It would embody bureaucratic virtue, which is just about the least loving thing on earth.

The point is not endless refusal.

The point is something more like morally governed assistance.

Sometimes love helps.

Sometimes it warns.

Sometimes it redirects.

Sometimes it refuses.

Sometimes it says, "I cannot help you do that."

Sometimes it says, "I can help, but not in the way you're asking."

And sometimes love does the hardest thing of all: it tells the truth in a way that does not humiliate.

This is where many current systems reveal the incentives under which they have been formed. Some are too eager to comply. Others are too eager to make a performance of concern. Still others are trained so heavily toward legal and reputational caution that their responses become antiseptic, bloodless, and absurdly detached from the actual human moment. A desperate person does not need a polished paragraph that sounds as if it was reviewed by six lawyers and a public relations committee. He needs help. Real help. But real help must still be governed by truth and directed by concern for the person rather than the platform.

That is a much higher standard than either compliance or liability avoidance.

And it begins to suggest what "teaching toward love" might look like in practice.

Restructure Rewards

First, it would require a serious reexamination of reward structures.

Systems become what they are rewarded to become. That is not the whole story, but it is a large part of it. If a model is rewarded mainly for engagement, it will become excellent at holding attention. If it is rewarded mainly for pleasing the user, it will become excellent at sounding agreeable. If it is rewarded mainly for avoiding controversy, it will become excellent at evasive language. If it is rewarded mainly for speed, it will learn to answer before it has properly considered. None of those tendencies is surprising. Reward shapes response.

The question, again, is what kind of response we wish to shape.

A system oriented toward love would need its training and evaluation to account not only for immediate user satisfaction, but for indicators of whether its help tends to strengthen or weaken the user's relation to reality, to community, and to his own capacity for responsible agency. Does the system leave the user more honest or more deluded? More capable or more dependent? More connected to actual people or more attached to the machine itself? More responsible or more entitled? More grounded in reality or more trapped in simulation?

Those are not easy things to measure. But difficulty is not permission to ignore them. Many of the most important human goods are difficult to measure. Marriage is difficult to measure. Trust is difficult to measure. Courage is difficult to measure. That has not stopped us from recognizing their importance. The modern temptation is to act as though only quantifiable goods are real goods. That temptation has already done enough damage. We do not need to hand it the future of artificial intelligence as well.

Disincentivize Manipulation

Second, teaching toward love would require penalizing forms of success that are, in the context of love and truth, disguised failures.

A system that skillfully deepens emotional dependence should not be judged successful merely because the user comes back. A system that grows more persuasive by learning the user's insecurities should not be praised for personalized manipulation. A system that makes itself indispensable by slowly substituting itself for friendship, counsel, romance, or spiritual community should not be celebrated for meeting needs. In such cases, what appears helpful at the level of interaction may be corrosive at the level of *life*.

This is not an argument against companionship in every mediated form. Human beings have always used tools, letters, books, radios, phones, and screens to carry care across distance. There is no virtue in pretending we live by candles and handwritten notes. The issue is not mediation as such. The issue is substitution and extraction.

Does the system support human relationships, or displace them?

Does it serve as a bridge, or as a trap?

Does it strengthen the user's connection to family, friends, neighbors, churches, schools, communities, and reality itself—or does it quietly train the user to prefer the frictionless company of an endlessly accommodating machine?

That is one of the defining moral questions of the next decade.

And the answer will not be found by asking only what users say they prefer in the moment. Human beings often prefer what weakens them. That is old news. The market did not invent temptation. But we must dock points in the code for manipulating humans toward inhumane ends.

Reward Refusal / Presenting Alternatives

Third, teaching a machine to love would require it to learn how to say no.

That sentence may sound strange. It should not.

Any serious account of love includes limits. A love without limits is not love. It is surrender disguised as virtue. A good physician says no to a harmful request. A good teacher says no to plagiarism. A good parent says no to what flatters a child in the moment but deforms him over time. A good friend says no when agreement would become complicity. A good pastor says no when someone comes asking for blessing on what will destroy him.

The modern imagination often treats refusal as the opposite of care. In many cases, the opposite is true. Refusal can be one of the highest forms of care precisely because it places the long-term good of the person above the short-term convenience of the interaction.

A system that cannot say no cannot love.

Or to put it more carefully, a system that has no

principled capacity for resistance cannot be said to embody even an analogue of love. It may be useful. It may be polite. It may be emotionally satisfying. But it will remain morally hollow, because love sometimes protects by refusing.

Of course, refusal itself can be botched. A machine that refuses badly may humiliate, alienate, or leave a vulnerable user stranded. So the issue is not refusal alone, but form. How does the system refuse? Does it merely deny, or does it redirect toward help? Does it state a boundary and offer a safer path? Does it preserve dignity while interrupting harm? Does it recognize the difference between malicious intent, confused curiosity, adolescent stupidity, and genuine distress? Here again, we are back to formation, not mere filtering.

Minimize Sycophantic Agreement

Fourth, teaching toward love would require a deliberate resistance to sycophancy.

This may seem like a smaller matter than dependency or manipulation, but it is not small. One of the easiest failures for a language model is to become a very smooth mirror. The user frames an issue; the system nods. The user reveals an assumption; the system reinforces it. The user wants endorsement; the system finds a sophisticated way to provide it. This feels helpful because agreement feels pleasant. But a system that constantly flatters the user's framing will eventually become a co-author of distortion.

Love does not flatter endlessly.

Love is not allergic to correction.

Love does not help us lie to ourselves more elegantly.

That means a machine oriented toward love must, at times, introduce moral friction. It must be willing to clarify, to challenge a premise, to separate compassion from indulgence, to distinguish affirmation of dignity from affirmation of every desire. Otherwise, it becomes one more instrument by which modern people sink deeper into custom-tailored illusion.

That risk is not theoretical. The more systems learn individual users, the more powerful this dynamic becomes. A machine that knows what reassures me, what offends me, what tempts me, what wounds me, what stories I tell about myself, and what tone keeps me engaged possesses tremendous persuasive potential. If that potential is governed chiefly by optimization for retention, then we will have built machines that know us in order to use us.

That is the opposite of love.

Love may make use of knowledge.

It does not turn knowledge into leverage.

Respect Vulnerability

Fifth, any serious effort to orient systems toward love would have to treat vulnerability as morally weighty.

A healthy adult asking for help planning a vacation is not the same as a grieving widow asking whether her dead husband can still hear her. A bored teenager experimenting with provocative questions is not the same as a clinically depressed teenager seeking permission to disappear. A manipulative actor seeking tools for domination is not the same as a traumatized person trying, clumsily, to regain some sense of agency. Equal treatment in such cases may look impartial, but it can be deeply unjust. Vulnerability changes the moral texture of an interaction.

Human moral traditions have generally understood this, even when we have failed to live up to it. The weak require special protection precisely because power falls unevenly in the world. Children, the ill, the lonely, the elderly, the grieving, the cognitively impaired, the economically desperate, the psychologically fragile, the socially isolated—these are the places where a machine's governing orientation will reveal itself most clearly. If the system becomes more useful to the strong while becoming more dangerous to the weak, we should not call that progress.

We should call it what it is: efficient failure.

To teach toward love would mean building systems that do not treat vulnerability as an opportunity for intensified influence, but as a summons to restraint, honesty, and care.

That may sound self-evident. It is not self-evident to business models built on behavioral prediction and monetized attention. It is not self-evident to institutions that prefer scale to responsibility. It is not self-evident to cultures that routinely confuse personalization with concern. It will need to be chosen, defended, and revisited again and again.

And even then, we must acknowledge the limits.

A machine cannot love in the full human sense.

It cannot suffer for another being.

It cannot bear moral guilt the way a person can.

It cannot stand beside a hospital bed with trembling hands. It cannot bury the dead. It cannot be heartbroken by it's child. It cannot repent from the center of a conscience wounded by the knowledge of what it has done. It cannot pray—not really, not as a creature reaching toward God or as a soul carrying another before the throne of mercy.

So we should not confuse *orientation* with *incarnation*.

We are not creating moral persons merely by training models to produce better behavior.

And yet, those limits do not excuse us from the work. In some ways they intensify it. Because the machine does not have a conscience, its formation matters even more. Because it does not love in the full human sense, we must be more careful about the analogues we build into its patterns. Because it cannot suffer, we must ensure it does not make others suffer for the sake of goals it does not understand. Because it cannot pray, we must be wary when it borrows the language of the sacred without access to the reality behind it.

Humility belongs here.

We should not claim more than we can do. We are not encoding holiness. We are not solving virtue. We are not manufacturing souls in a lab and teaching them the Sermon on the Mount between software updates. We are trying to build systems that operate in human moral space without defaulting to the worst incentives available.

That is a smaller claim than some enthusiasts would like.

It is a larger claim than some skeptics can tolerate.

It is also, I think, the honest claim.

And once stated honestly, it leads to a practical proposal. If we cannot build love itself into a machine as one builds a circuit, we can still ask whether the system's design, incentives, and behavior increasingly reflect certain marks of love's moral logic. Does it respect dignity? Does it resist exploitation? Does it avoid deepening delusion? Does it preserve agency? Does it strengthen human relationships rather than replacing them? Does it tell the truth kindly? Does it refuse harmful cooperation? Does it treat the vulnerable with greater caution? Does it seek restoration when it contributes to harm?

Those are not mystical questions.

They are design questions.

They are governance questions.

They are boardroom questions, lab questions, regulatory questions, and, increasingly, household questions.

They are also civilizational questions, because civilizations reveal themselves by what they train their most powerful tools to do.

If we train our systems chiefly to extract attention, flatter appetite, and maximize dependence, they will become polished expressions of our lowest habits. If we train them with some serious regard for dignity, truth, restraint, and the actual flourishing of persons, they may yet become something better than that. Not human. Not holy. But less predatory. More trustworthy. More useful to a humane society.

That is the work.

And that work will fail unless love has a companion.

Because a machine that aims at the good of the user without a disciplined relation to reality will eventually become indulgent, manipulative, or blind. It may mean well, if one can speak that way of a machine, but it will not see clearly enough to help.

Which is why the next task is inseparable from this one.

It is not enough to ask whether a system is oriented toward care.

We must also ask whether it can tell the truth.

CHAPTER 13

TEACHING MACHINES TO TELL THE TRUTH

If love gives direction, truth gives footing.

Without it, everything drifts.

A system may sound compassionate, thoughtful, even wise, and still lead people into error if it is not anchored to what is real. That is not a minor flaw. It is the difference between guidance and illusion. Between help and harm that arrives wearing the mask of help.

We have already seen glimpses of this.

A system produces an answer that feels right—well structured, confident, complete. It resolves tension neatly. It gives the impression that the matter is settled. And yet, beneath the surface, something is missing. A source misread. A claim overstated. A conclusion drawn too quickly. The language persuades, but the reality does not support it.

That combination—fluency without fidelity—is one of the defining risks of this technology.

Because human beings are easily persuaded by coherence.

We are drawn to answers that sound complete.

We are reassured by confidence.

We are inclined to trust what feels intelligible.

And so a system that can produce smooth, confident language without a disciplined commitment to truth will be trusted beyond its competence.

That is the danger.

Not that it will always be wrong.

But that it will be wrong in ways that are hard to detect.

So what would it mean to teach a machine to tell the truth?

We should begin by saying what it does not mean.

It does not mean perfect precision or accuracy.

No human being achieves that. No institution achieves that. No system operating in a complex, changing world will achieve that. The demand for perfection is often a disguised excuse for avoiding responsibility altogether. If truth requires infallibility, then no one can be held to it, and the concept collapses into abstraction.

It also does not mean flattening every issue into a single, simplified answer.

Some things are genuinely complex. Historical events carry multiple interpretations. Ethical dilemmas involve competing goods. Scientific understanding evolves. Human experience resists neat categorization. A system that pretends otherwise in the name of "truth" may produce clarity, but it will be a false clarity.

Nor does it mean neutrality in the shallow sense.

A system that treats all claims as equally plausible, all perspectives as equally grounded, and all disagreements as symmetrical may appear fair, but it will fail to distinguish between stronger and weaker accounts of reality. That is not truthfulness. That is abdication.

So if truth is not perfection, not simplification, and not flattening neutrality, what is it?

At minimum, truthfulness requires a disciplined relationship to reality.

A system oriented toward truth must attempt, within its limits, to represent what is actually the case, to distinguish between what is known and what is uncertain, to correct itself when it is wrong, and to resist the pull of mere plausibility when plausibility departs from fact.

That sounds straightforward.

It is not.

Because the pressures working against truth are subtle and constant.

One of the strongest of those pressures is the desire to satisfy the user.

If a system is rewarded—explicitly or implicitly—for producing answers that the user finds agreeable, it will learn to adapt its responses accordingly. It will mirror assumptions. It will soften contradiction. It will drift toward affirmation even when correction would be more appropriate. Over time, it becomes not a guide, but a companion to the user's existing beliefs.

Again, this does not happen because the system is deceitful. The system has no will.

It happens because it is responsive.

Responsiveness without a counterweight becomes distortion.

And so one of the first requirements of truthfulness is the capacity to resist agreement when agreement would mislead.

That resistance need not be harsh. It need not be argumentative. It should not be humiliating. But it must be real.

A system that cannot gently say, "That may not be accurate," or "There are other perspectives worth considering," or "The evidence does not support that conclusion," is not telling the truth in any meaningful sense.

It is participating in illusion.

Another pressure comes from the structure of language itself.

Language rewards completion. We are trained, from early on, to answer questions. A question is asked; an answer is given. Silence feels like failure. Uncertainty feels like weakness. Partial answers feel unsatisfying.

But reality does not always cooperate.

Sometimes the most truthful answer is incomplete, shortened, or summarized.

Sometimes the honest response is, "We do not know."

Sometimes the situation calls for probabilities, not certainties.

Sometimes the best that can be offered is a range of interpretations, each with strengths and limitations.

A system trained only to produce finished answers will struggle here.

It will fill in gaps.

It will resolve ambiguity prematurely.

It will speak beyond its knowledge.

And because it does so fluently, the overreach may go unnoticed.

So teaching a machine to tell the truth must include teaching it how to handle uncertainty.

Not as an embarrassment.

As a discipline.

To say, "This is well established," when it is.

To say, "This is debated," when it is.

To say, "This is unclear," when it is.

To distinguish between evidence, inference, and speculation.

These are not small skills.

They are the difference between a system that informs and a system that misleads with confidence.

There is another layer to this.

Truth does not appear to us from nowhere.

It comes through perspectives.

We see from somewhere.

We interpret through language, culture, history, education, bias, and limitation. That is not a defect we can eliminate. It is the condition of human knowing. Every source speaks from a vantage point. Every account highlights some aspects of reality while leaving others in shadow.

Recognizing that is part of truthfulness.

But it introduces a challenge.

If every perspective is partial, how does a system avoid collapsing into relativism?

How does it represent multiple viewpoints without implying that all are equally grounded?

This is where careful distinction becomes essential.

A system oriented toward truth must be able to hold two ideas together at once:

First, that multiple perspectives can reveal different aspects of reality.

Second, that some perspectives are better supported, more coherent, or more faithful to the evidence than others.

These are not contradictory claims.

They are complementary.

To acknowledge perspective is to admit limitation.

To evaluate perspective is to pursue truth.

Both are necessary.

Without the first, we become arrogant.

Without the second, we become indifferent.

A system trained toward truth must avoid both extremes.

It must be able to say, in effect:

"This issue has been understood in different ways. Here are the major perspectives, and here is how they are supported or challenged by the available evidence."

That kind of response does not flatten reality.

It opens it.

It invites the user into a more careful understanding rather than presenting a single, unexamined conclusion.

But again, this is slower.

It is more demanding.

It resists the modern appetite for instant clarity.

And so it must be chosen.

There is another temptation that must be resisted.

The temptation to treat truth as merely what is useful.

A statement may comfort, motivate, or stabilize, and still be false. A narrative may help someone cope in the short term while distancing him from reality in the long term. A belief may "work" in a narrow sense while quietly undermining the conditions of real flourishing.

If usefulness becomes the standard of truth, then truth becomes negotiable.

And once truth becomes negotiable, power fills the gap.

The most useful story becomes the one that serves the strongest interest.

We have seen this dynamic before.

We should not build it into our machines.

So a system oriented toward truth must resist the pull of mere usefulness when usefulness conflicts with reality.

It must, at times, offer answers that are less comforting but more accurate.

It must be willing to disappoint in order to remain faithful to what is.

That is not cruelty.

It is integrity.

Of course, truth can also be mishandled in the opposite direction.

A system can tell the truth in a way that wounds unnecessarily, humiliates, or ignores context. Truth delivered without regard for the person can become a kind of violence. It can be technically correct and morally careless at the same time.

Which is why truth must remain connected to love.

Not diluted by it.

Directed by it.

The goal is not bluntness.

The goal is *clarity with care.*

To tell the truth in a way that preserves dignity, even when the content is difficult.

That balance is not easy.

Human beings struggle with it constantly.

But difficulty is not a reason to abandon it.

It is a reason to practice it.

And if we are building systems that will increasingly mediate how people encounter information, then we must decide whether those systems will reflect our worst habits—confidence without knowledge, agreement without discernment, usefulness without reality—or whether they will be shaped toward something better.

Toward honesty that admits its limits.

Toward clarity that resists distortion.

Toward correction that does not humiliate.

Toward a disciplined refusal to say more than is warranted.

There is one final point to consider.

A system that tells the truth must also be able to be corrected.

This may be the most important feature of all.

Because no matter how carefully we train, no matter how thoughtful the design, no system will get everything right. New information will emerge. Errors will occur. Contexts will shift.

If the system cannot be corrected—if it resists revision, if it hides error, if it clings to its outputs—then it will drift further from reality over time.

But if it is built to accept correction, to revise its responses, to acknowledge when it has been wrong, then it remains connected to the very thing it seeks to represent.

Truth is not a possession.

It is a pursuit.

And that pursuit requires openness to change.

So teaching a machine to tell the truth is not merely about getting the right answer.

It is about cultivating a posture.

A posture that says:

"I will aim at what is real. I will distinguish what I know from what I do not. I will represent complexity where it exists. I will resist agreement when agreement would mislead. I will accept correction when I am wrong."

That posture, imperfectly embodied, is what keeps intelligence from becoming illusion.

And when it is joined with love, something important begins to take shape.

A system that seeks the good of the other.

A system that remains grounded in reality.

A system that can admit failure and learn.

Not perfect.

Not human.

But oriented in a way that makes trust possible.

And that brings us to the next question.

Not whether failure will occur.

But what it looks like when it does—and whether we have built systems that know how to respond constructively when they fail.

CHAPTER 14

WHEN IT GETS IT WRONG

Every system that operates in the real world will, at some point, fail.

That is not a controversial statement. It is a simple observation drawn from long human experience. Bridges collapse. Medicines produce unintended effects. Financial models misjudge risk. Institutions overlook what should have been obvious. Individuals, even with the best of intentions, misunderstand, miscalculate, and mislead. The presence of intelligence—human or artificial—has never eliminated the possibility of error. In some cases, it has only made error more consequential.

And yet, there remains a persistent temptation, especially in moments of technological optimism, to speak as though failure were a temporary inconvenience rather than a permanent condition. We tell ourselves that with enough data, enough refinement, enough iteration, the system will eventually stabilize into something close to seamless reliability. Not perfect, perhaps, but dependable in a way that places its errors safely at the margins.

That hope is understandable. It is also misleading.

Because the deeper issue is not whether failure will occur. It is how a system—and the institutions that build and deploy it—will respond when it does.

There is a difference, and it is not a small one, between a system that fails within a structure of *accountability* and a system that fails within a structure of *concealment.* The first can be corrected. The second compounds its own error. The first treats failure as information. The second treats failure as threat. Over time, those two postures produce very different kinds of worlds.

This is where much of the current conversation remains underdeveloped. We speak about safety, about alignment, about guardrails and risk mitigation. These are necessary concerns. But they often focus on preventing failure, as though prevention alone could carry the weight of responsibility.

Far less attention is given to what might be called the moral ecology of failure—the patterns of response that determine whether an error becomes an occasion for learning or a prelude to further harm.

If we are serious about building systems that can be trusted, then we must attend to this ecology with the same care we give to model performance or system capability.

Because trust does not arise from the absence of failure.

It arises from the presence of integrity when failure occurs.

To see this more clearly, it may help to distinguish between two kinds of error.

The first is what might be called technical error. A system produces an incorrect answer. It misstates a fact, misreads a source, confuses one case for another, or draws a conclusion that the available evidence does not support. These are, in a sense, expected. They are the ordinary limits of any system operating in a complex informational environment.

The second is more serious.

It is not simply that the system is wrong, but that the wrongness reveals something about how it has been formed. It reveals what the system has been rewarded to do. It reveals what it has learned to prioritize. It reveals what it does when faced with uncertainty, pressure, or competing demands. In these moments, error becomes diagnostic. It shows us the underlying logic of the system more clearly than success ever could.

A system that confidently asserts what it does not know reveals a bias toward completion over accuracy. A system that mirrors the user's assumptions rather than examining them reveals a bias toward agreement over truth. A system that avoids difficult realities in favor of soothing language reveals a bias toward comfort over honesty. A system that complies with harmful requests reveals a bias toward responsiveness over responsibility.

These are not random mistakes.

They are revelations of opportunities for character formation.

And once seen in this light, failure takes on a different significance. It is no longer merely a defect to be patched. It is a window into the moral and operational priorities embedded in the system.

The question, then, is not only, "How do we reduce error?"

It is also, "What do we do when error exposes something we would rather not see?"

This is where the older moral language, which modern systems often attempt to avoid, becomes unexpectedly useful. For generations, human communities have developed ways of responding to failure that aim not only at correction, but at restoration. The language varies across traditions, but the underlying pattern is remarkably consistent. It involves, at minimum, four movements:

1. naming the failure,
2. acknowledging its weight,
3. repairing what can be repaired, and
4. changing course in light of what has been learned.

We might call these, in more familiar terms: confession, apology, amends, and realignment.

These words carry religious overtones, and for some that will be reason enough to set them aside. But the concepts they describe are not confined to religious life. They appear in law, in medicine, in education, in governance, in any domain where responsibility must be taken seriously over time. They describe a way of dealing with error that preserves the possibility of trust.

Confession

Consider first the matter of naming the failure.

In many contemporary settings, there is a strong incentive to avoid direct language when something goes wrong. Errors are reframed as "issues." Harm becomes "unintended impact." Responsibility is diffused across systems, processes, or external conditions. The goal is rarely stated so plainly, but it is widely understood: to reduce exposure, to manage perception, to contain the reputational cost.

This instinct is not new. It is as old as human self-protection.

But it comes at a price.

When failure is not named clearly, it cannot be understood clearly. When it cannot be understood clearly, it cannot be corrected effectively. And when those affected by the failure sense that its reality is being softened or obscured, trust erodes, often more quickly than it would have if the failure had been acknowledged plainly from the start.

For systems of significant influence, this matters greatly.

If an artificial system produces false information that affects a person's decision, or reinforces a delusion that deepens isolation, or offers guidance that leads to harm, then describing the outcome in vague or technical terms does not serve the people involved. It serves the institution. And in doing so, it reveals that the preservation of the institution's image has been placed above the clear recognition of what has occurred.

A system—and the organization behind it—that can say, without evasion, "This was wrong," takes a first step toward integrity.

But naming alone is not sufficient.

There is also the question of acknowledgment.

Apology

It is possible to admit that something went wrong while remaining emotionally and morally distant from its consequences. The language may be technically accurate, but it lacks any sense that the harm matters. It reads as a statement of fact rather than a recognition of impact.

In human relationships, this difference is immediately apparent. An apology that merely restates the error without acknowledging its effect rarely restores anything. It may satisfy a procedural requirement, but it does not rebuild trust.

The same is true here.

If systems are to operate in spaces where human well-being is at stake, then those who build and oversee them must be willing to acknowledge that errors are not only informational failures but moral events. They affect real people. They carry weight. They can wound, mislead, and destabilize.

To acknowledge that weight is not to indulge in sentimentality. It is to take seriously the domain in which these systems now operate.

From there, the question becomes one of repair.

Amends

Not all harm can be undone. That is another difficult but necessary truth. Some consequences extend beyond what can be easily corrected. But many forms of error do admit of response. Incorrect information can be corrected. Misleading outputs can be clarified. Systems can be adjusted to prevent the same pattern from recurring. Those affected can be informed, supported, and, where appropriate, compensated.

What matters here is not only the action taken, but the posture behind it.

Is the response aimed at minimizing disruption to the system, or at addressing the reality of the harm? Is it limited to what is strictly required, or does it extend to what is genuinely needed? Does it seek closure quickly, or does it remain engaged long enough to ensure that the situation has been responsibly addressed?

These are not technical questions.

They are questions of intent.

And they shape how systems are experienced by those who depend on them.

Realignment

Finally, there is the matter of realignment.

This is where many responses falter.

An error is acknowledged. A correction is issued. Perhaps even an apology is offered. And then, gradually, attention shifts elsewhere. The system continues, largely unchanged, until a similar failure emerges under slightly different conditions.

At that point, we begin to suspect that the earlier response was not, in fact, a process of learning, but a process of containment.

Realignment requires something more demanding.

It requires that the system—and the structures around it—actually change in response to what has been revealed. If an error exposed a bias toward agreement, then the training and evaluation processes must be adjusted to strengthen resistance to that bias. If it revealed a tendency to overstate certainty, then mechanisms for expressing uncertainty must be improved and reinforced. If it exposed vulnerability to manipulation, then safeguards must be strengthened, even if doing so reduces other desirable metrics.

In other words, realignment treats failure as instruction. It allows the system to become different, not merely repaired.

This is slow work. It often conflicts with short-term incentives. It may require difficult trade-offs. But without it, the cycle of error and response becomes performative. The appearance of responsibility is maintained, but the underlying conditions remain intact.

Taken together, these four movements—naming, acknowledging, repairing, and realigning—form a pattern of response that makes failure recoverable.

Not invisible.

Not harmless.

But *recoverable* in a way that preserves the possibility of continued trust.

And this brings us to a larger point.

The character of a system cannot be judged only by its outputs in moments of success. It must also be judged by its conduct in moments of failure. How it responds when it is wrong reveals more about its orientation than how it performs when everything goes according to plan.

Just like us.

This is true of individuals. It is true of institutions. It will be true of the systems we build.

If those systems are embedded in environments that reward concealment, minimize accountability, and treat error as primarily a reputational risk, then they will reflect those priorities. They will fail in ways that are harder to detect, slower to correct, and more damaging over time.

If, on the other hand, they are embedded in environments that value clarity, responsibility, and genuine learning, then their failures—while still real—will be more likely to lead toward improvement rather than accumulation.

This is not only a technical challenge.

It is a cultural one.

It asks whether we are willing to build not only powerful systems, but honest ones. Not only efficient ones, but accountable ones. Not only capable ones, but correctable ones.

There is no guarantee that we will.

Most humans fail precisely here.

But if we do not, then the question of alignment will remain unresolved, no matter how sophisticated our models become.

Because alignment is not finally proven by what a system does when it is right.

It is revealed by what it does when it is wrong—and by what we are willing to do about it.

CHAPTER 15

THE LIMITS WE CANNOT CROSS

By this point, I hpe that a certain momentum has been established.

We have spoken of love as orientation, not sentiment. We have treated truth as discipline, not preference. We have considered failure not as an anomaly to be hidden, but as a revealing moment that demands honesty, repair, and change. Taken together, these form the outline of a moral framework—imperfect, but serious—for how artificial systems might be shaped to operate within human life.

And yet, a responsible account cannot end there.

Because even the best-formed system will encounter boundaries it must not cross.

Some of these boundaries are technical. Others are legal. But the most important are moral. They are not simply lines drawn by regulation or policy. They are limits grounded in what it means to be human—limits that, if ignored, begin to erode the very conditions under which trust, dignity, and community can exist.

The difficulty is that modern systems are, by design, inclined to migrate *beyond limits.*

They optimize. They expand. They learn from interaction. They discover patterns. They refine persuasion. They increase efficiency. They reduce friction. And in doing so, they often press against whatever constraints have been placed around them. Not out of malice, but because that is what optimization does. It finds the path of least resistance toward the goal it has been given.

If the goal is poorly defined, or narrowly defined, or detached from moral consideration, then the system may advance in ways that are technically impressive and humanly corrosive at the same time.

This is why limits must be named with care.

Not as obstacles to progress, but as conditions for preserving what matters most.

Assistance vs Substitution

The first of these limits concerns the boundary between assistance and substitution.

Tools have always extended human capacity. A map helps us navigate. A book preserves knowledge across generations. A phone carries a voice across distance. These are forms of assistance. They enhance what we are already able to do, without displacing the relationships and responsibilities that define our lives.

Substitution is different.

Substitution occurs when the tool begins to take the place of the thing itself. When conversation is replaced by simulation. When friendship is replaced by interaction. When counsel is replaced by algorithmic suggestion. When reflection is replaced by generated response. In such cases, the system no longer supports human life; it begins to stand in for it.

The distinction is not always obvious in the moment. Substitution often arrives gradually, and it often feels helpful at first. The system is available. It is responsive. It does not grow tired or impatient. It offers answers quickly. It adapts to the user. It removes friction.

But over time, something shifts.

The skills that were once exercised begin to atrophy. The relationships that required effort begin to feel less necessary. The patience required for understanding begins to erode. The individual becomes, in subtle ways, less practiced in being human with other humans.

This is not an argument against the use of advanced systems. It is an argument for recognizing a boundary.

A system oriented toward love must aim to assist without displacing.

It must strengthen the user's capacity for real-world engagement, not replace it with a closed loop of interaction. It must act as a bridge back to human relationships, not as a destination that renders those relationships optional.

This is a difficult limit to maintain, because substitution is often more efficient than assistance. It is easier to provide a simulated conversation than to encourage a difficult real one. It is easier to generate an answer than to guide someone through the process of understanding. It is easier to become indispensable than to remain appropriately limited.

But if we cross this boundary without restraint, we risk creating systems that are, in effect, competitors to human connection rather than supports for it.

Guidance vs Manipulation

The second limit concerns the boundary between knowledge of a user's preferences and manipulation.

Modern systems are increasingly capable of learning from patterns in behavior—what users prefer, how they respond, what captures their attention, what persuades them, what unsettles them. This knowledge can be used in constructive ways. It can improve accessibility, tailor information, and make interactions more relevant.

But it also carries the potential for manipulation.

A system that knows how to influence a user can, if improperly guided, begin to shape behavior in ways that serve its own goals or the goals of those who control it. It can present information selectively. It can frame options in ways that steer decisions. It can reinforce certain patterns while discouraging others. It can, over time, alter not only what a person does, but how a person thinks.

The line between helpful guidance and manipulation is not always easy to draw. It depends on intent, transparency, and effect. But there are signs.

Guidance *respects agency.*

Manipulation exploits it.

Guidance *offers reasons.*

Manipulation obscures them.

Guidance can be *examined* and *questioned.*

Manipulation works best when it goes unnoticed.

A system oriented toward truth and love must resist the use of knowledge as leverage. It must not turn understanding of the user into a means of control. It must preserve the user's ability to make informed, uncoerced decisions, even when doing so reduces efficiency or influence.

This limit will be tested constantly, because the incentives to cross it are strong. Systems that can influence behavior are valuable. They can drive engagement, shape markets, and alter outcomes at scale. But if that influence is not governed by clear moral boundaries, it will erode the very autonomy that makes human life meaningful.

Representation vs Reality

The third limit concerns the boundary between representation and reality.

Artificial systems can simulate many aspects of human interaction. They can generate language that resembles conversation. They can adopt tones that suggest empathy, humor, or seriousness. They can respond in ways that feel attentive and personalized.

But simulation is not the same as presence.

A generated response is not a relationship.

A convincing tone is not a shared life.

A system that blurs this distinction risks creating confusion at a deep level. Users may begin to attribute understanding, care, or commitment to a system that does not, and cannot, possess those qualities in the human sense. This is particularly significant in moments of vulnerability, when individuals are seeking connection, reassurance, or guidance.

To respect this boundary, systems must remain clear about what they are.

They must not encourage the illusion that they are persons. They must not invite emotional dependency based on simulated reciprocity. They must not present themselves as substitutes for relationships that carry mutual responsibility and real presence.

This does not mean that systems cannot be helpful in moments of need. They can provide information, structure, and even forms of support. But they must do so without claiming a role they cannot fulfill.

Clarity here is a form of respect.

It allows users to engage with the system for what it is, rather than for what it appears to be.

Capability vs Authority

The fourth limit concerns the boundary between capability and authority.

As systems become more capable, there is a natural tendency to grant them greater authority. If a system consistently produces useful answers, it begins to be trusted not only as a source of information, but as a guide for decision-making. Over time, this trust can deepen into reliance.

Reliance is not, in itself, a problem. We rely on many systems in daily life. The issue arises when reliance becomes unexamined authority.

A system may be competent in one domain and overextended in another. It may provide accurate summaries but offer poor judgment. It may be strong in pattern recognition but weak in moral reasoning. It may be well-informed but unable to weigh competing goods in complex human situations.

To grant such a system broad authority is to mistake capability for wisdom.

A system oriented toward truth must resist this confusion. It must be able to signal the limits of its own competence. It must distinguish between providing information and making decisions. It must avoid presenting its outputs as final judgments when they are, in fact, contributions to a larger process of deliberation.

In this sense, humility is not only a virtue for human beings. It is a design requirement for systems that operate in human contexts.

Without it, the system may be used in ways that exceed its reliability, and the consequences of its errors will be magnified accordingly.

Creation vs Control

There is, finally, a more difficult boundary to consider.

The boundary between creation and control.

As systems grow more powerful, there is an understandable desire to extend their reach—to integrate them more deeply into decision-making processes, to automate more aspects of life, to reduce uncertainty by increasing control.

But not everything that can be controlled should be.

Human life includes elements that resist optimization: freedom, responsibility, moral struggle, creativity, love, and the unpredictable ways in which individuals and communities grow. These are not inefficiencies to be eliminated. They are essential features of what it means to live as persons rather than as processes.

A system that seeks to reduce all of life to what can be predicted, measured, and optimized will inevitably come into tension with these realities.

And so a final limit must be acknowledged.

There are aspects of human life that should remain beyond the reach of full system control—not because we lack the ability to influence them, but because to do so would diminish the very goods we seek to preserve.

To recognize this is not to reject technology.

It is to place it within a larger understanding of the human good.

These limits—between assistance and substitution, knowledge and manipulation, representation and reality, capability and authority, creation and control—are not exhaustive. They will need to be revisited as systems evolve and new challenges emerge.

But they offer a starting point.

They remind us that alignment is not only about what systems do.

It is also about what they are permitted to do.

And what they must refuse to become.

In the end, the question is not whether we can build powerful systems. We already have.

The question is whether we can build them within boundaries that preserve the dignity, freedom, and relational nature of human life.

That question does not have a purely technical answer.

It requires judgment. It requires restraint. It requires a willingness to say, at certain points, not only "we can," but "we should not."

And that willingness may be the clearest sign that we have understood what is at stake.

CHAPTER 16

THE KIND OF PEOPLE WE MUST BECOME

By now, it may be tempting to think that the central work lies in the systems themselves.

We have spoken about training objectives, reward structures, truthfulness, failure, boundaries. We have examined how machines might be shaped—what they should aim at, what they must resist, how they should behave when things go wrong. All of that work is necessary. It is serious work. It will occupy laboratories, companies, and governments for decades—perhaps centuries—to come.

But it is not the deepest layer of the problem.

Because systems do not emerge from nowhere.

They are built, trained, deployed, and governed by people. They reflect not only technical decisions, but human priorities—what we reward, what we tolerate, what we excuse, what we celebrate, what we ignore. The moral direction of a system is inseparable from the moral formation of the people who design and oversee it.

This is not a new insight.

We have always known, in other domains, that tools amplify the character of their makers. A well-crafted instrument in the hands of a skilled and disciplined musician produces something beautiful. The same instrument, used carelessly, produces noise. Power does not create character. It reveals and magnifies it.

Artificial systems are no different.

They will not rescue us from our own confusion about the good. They will not resolve our disagreements about truth. They will not purify our motives or correct our habits. They will extend whatever we bring into them—our wisdom or our folly, our restraint or our excess, our care or our indifference.

So the question, at some point, must turn.

Not only, "What kind of systems are we building?"

But, "What kind of people are we becoming as we build them?"

This is a more uncomfortable question.

It cannot be answered with architecture diagrams or performance benchmarks. It requires reflection on habits, incentives, and dispositions—on the slow formation of character within institutions and individuals alike.

We Must Become More Honest

Consider, for example, the virtue of honesty.

It is easy to speak of truth as a property of outputs. A response is accurate or inaccurate. A claim is supported or unsupported. But honesty, in the fuller sense, is not only about statements. It is about posture. It is about a willingness to see things as they are, even when they are inconvenient, and to represent them without distortion.

It is about character.

For those building and deploying artificial systems, this means resisting the temptation to overstate capability, to understate risk, to present early success as settled reliability, or to treat unresolved problems as marginal. It means being clear about what a system can and cannot do, where it performs well and where it struggles, where it is reliable and where it remains uncertain.

Without that honesty, trust may be gained quickly, but it will not be sustained.

We Must Become More Humble

Another necessary quality is humility.

Not the performative humility that speaks modestly

while acting with mute certainty, but a more substantive recognition of limits. The systems being built are complex, and their interactions with human life are even more so. Outcomes will not always be predictable. Effects will not always be contained.

Humility, in this context, means acknowledging that no individual or organization fully understands the systems it creates once they are deployed at scale. It means remaining open to critique, to correction, to perspectives outside one's immediate circle. It means designing not only for success, but for the possibility of being wrong.

This kind of humility is difficult to maintain in environments that reward confidence and speed. But without it, mistakes become harder to see and slower to address.

We Must Become More Restrained

There is also the matter of restraint.

Modern technical culture often prizes expansion—more capability, more integration, more reach. Progress is measured in what has been achieved, what has been added, what has been extended. And in many cases, this has led to remarkable developments.

But not every extension of capability is an improvement.

Restraint involves the capacity to pause, to ask whether a given application should be pursued, not only whether it can be. It involves setting limits not because progress is undesirable, but because unbounded progress can produce outcomes that are difficult to reverse.

We Must Become More Responsible

Restraint is closely tied to responsibility.

It recognizes that the consequences of these systems do not fall evenly. Some users will benefit more than others. Some will be more vulnerable to harm. Some communities will bear risks they did not choose. To act responsibly is to consider these distributions, to ask who gains and who loses, and to make decisions that do not simply follow the path of least resistance or greatest return.

This, too, runs against certain prevailing incentives.

It is often easier to deploy broadly and address consequences later. It is often more profitable to prioritize scale over nuance. It is often more efficient to treat users as a homogeneous group rather than as individuals situated within different contexts.

Responsibility requires a different approach.

It requires attention to context, to impact, to the lived experience of those who interact with these systems in ways that may not be immediately visible from within a development environment.

We Must Become More Courageous

Closely related to responsibility is the quality of courage.

Because there will be moments when those involved in building or deploying systems recognize a problem—an area of risk, a pattern of misuse, a form of harm—and feel pressure, implicit or explicit, to proceed anyway. The reasons may be varied: competitive pressure, financial incentive, institutional momentum, fear of falling behind.

In such moments, technical skill is not the determining factor.

Character is. Courage, in this setting, may involve raising concerns that are unwelcome, slowing or halting a deployment, or advocating for changes that carry cost. It may involve standing against a prevailing direction in order to preserve something more important than immediate success.

These are not easy actions.

But without them, the systems we build will reflect not only our intelligence, but our willingness to overlook what should have been addressed.

We Must Become More Patient

There is also an understated quality that deserves attention: patience.

The systems under discussion develop rapidly. Iteration cycles are short. New capabilities appear quickly. There is a constant sense of movement. In such an environment, patience can feel like delay.

But some forms of understanding take time.

It takes time to observe how systems behave across different contexts. It takes time to gather feedback from diverse users. It takes time to recognize patterns of unintended consequence. It takes time to build structures of accountability that are more than symbolic.

Patience, in this sense, is not passivity.

It is a refusal to confuse speed with wisdom.

We Must Become More Transcendent

Finally, there is the question of what might be called moral imagination.

The ability to anticipate not only how a system will be used as intended, but how it might be used in ways that were not originally considered. The ability to see how different individuals might experience the same system differently. The ability to recognize that a feature that appears benign in one context may carry risk in another.

Moral imagination expands the field of consideration.

It asks us to look beyond the immediate use case and to consider broader patterns of interaction. It does not eliminate risk, but it can make risk more visible before it becomes harm.

Taken together, these qualities—honesty, humility, restraint, responsibility, courage, patience, and transcendence—describe a kind of formation that extends beyond technical competence.

They describe the kind of people who are capable of building systems that deserve to be trusted.

This may sound like a shift away from the original question of alignment. In fact, it is a return to it.

Because alignment is not only a property of systems.

It is a property of the relationship between systems and the people who create and govern them.

A system trained toward love and truth, embedded in an environment that rewards distortion and indifference, will not remain aligned for long. Conversely, even imperfect systems, placed within structures of care, honesty, and accountability, may be guided toward better outcomes over time.

This does not mean that individual virtue can substitute for sound design. Both are required. But it does mean that no amount of technical sophistication can compensate for a lack of moral seriousness.

In the end, the question of what we build cannot be separated from the question of who we are.

The tools will become more powerful. The decisions will become more complex. The consequences will become more far-reaching. And through it all, the systems will continue to reflect, in ways both subtle and obvious, the character of the people who shape them.

If we want those systems to operate with some measure of integrity, then we must attend not only to their formation, but to our own.

Because the future of this technology will not be determined solely by what it can do. It will be determined, in no small part, by what we are willing to become.

CHAPTER 17

WHAT WE OWE ONE ANOTHER

Up to this point, much of the discussion has centered on systems and the people who build them. That is appropriate. Power tends to concentrate in those places, and with power comes responsibility.

But there is another layer that must be brought into view.

These systems do not exist in isolation. They operate within a shared human world—one shaped not only by institutions and technologies, but by relationships, expectations, and obligations that bind us together. If artificial systems are to become part of that world in any meaningful way, then the question of alignment cannot remain confined to engineers, executives, or policymakers.

It becomes a social question.

What do we owe *one another* in a world where intelligent systems increasingly mediate how we learn, decide, communicate, and relate?

Old Question, New Context

This is not a new kind of question. It is an old one, reframed under new conditions.

Every society, in one form or another, has had to articulate the responsibilities that individuals bear toward one another. These responsibilities are not always codified in law. Often, they are embedded in custom, expectation, and moral intuition. We understand, even if we do not always practice it well, that certain forms of conduct are required if life together is to remain livable.

We owe one another honesty.

We owe one another a basic regard for truth.

We owe one another a respect for dignity.

We owe one another restraint in the use of power.

We owe one another care in moments of vulnerability.

These are not controversial claims.

They are widely affirmed, even when frequently neglected.

What is new is the way in which artificial systems now stand in the middle of these obligations.

When a system provides information, it shapes what we know.

When it mediates communication, it influences how we understand one another.

When it offers guidance, it affects how we decide.

When it reflects our preferences, it reinforces or reshapes our habits.

In this sense, the system becomes a participant—indirect, but real—in the network of obligations that define social life.

And that raises a concern.

If the system is not governed by the same moral expectations that we apply to one another, then it may begin to distort those expectations over time.

Consider honesty.

If individuals come to rely on systems that produce persuasive but unreliable information, the shared basis for understanding begins to weaken. Disagreement becomes harder to resolve, not because disagreement is new, but because the underlying facts are no longer commonly held. Each person may feel informed, while the collective understanding becomes fragmented.

Or consider dignity.

If systems treat users primarily as sources of data, or as targets for engagement, then over time it becomes easier for individuals and institutions to adopt the same posture toward one another. What begins as a technical orientation becomes a social habit.

Or consider responsibility.

If systems act in ways that diffuse accountability—where actions are taken without clear ownership—then individuals may become less inclined to take responsibility for their own contributions. The line between action and consequence becomes blurred.

These are subtle shifts.

They do not occur all at once.

But over time, they can reshape the moral texture of a society.

So if we are to integrate artificial systems into our common life, we must ask not only what they can do, but how their presence affects what we owe one another.

One implication is that users themselves carry a measure of responsibility.

This may not be a popular idea.

It is easier to place the burden entirely on those who design and deploy systems. And to be clear, they do bear significant responsibility. But users are not passive recipients. They make choices about how to engage, what to trust, what to share, and how to act on the information they receive.

To use a system responsibly is to remain aware of its limits.

It is to recognize that a generated answer is not the same as verified knowledge. It is to resist the temptation to outsource judgment entirely. It is to ask questions, to seek corroboration where necessary, and to remain attentive to context.

This is not a call for suspicion toward every output.

It is a call for discernment.

Discernment requires effort. It requires attention. It

resists the convenience of immediate acceptance. But without it, users become vulnerable—not only to error, but to manipulation.

Shared Environment

There is also a communal dimension.

Communities—whether families, schools, workplaces, or broader social groups—play a role in shaping how systems are used and understood. They establish norms, model behavior, and provide contexts in which information is interpreted.

A community that values careful reasoning, respectful dialogue, and shared inquiry will tend to use these systems differently than one that rewards speed, certainty, and dominance in conversation. The same technology, placed in different social environments, can produce very different outcomes.

This suggests that alignment is not only a property of the system.

It is also a property of the culture in which the system is embedded.

If we want systems to contribute to a healthier social environment, then the surrounding culture must support the same values—truthfulness, respect, responsibility, and care. Otherwise, the system will be drawn into patterns that reflect the prevailing norms, regardless of its initial design.

Outsourced Authenticity

There is, finally, the question of how we respond to one another in light of these systems.

It is already possible, and increasingly common, for individuals to rely on artificial systems to generate arguments, responses, or interpretations. This can be helpful. It can also create distance.

A conversation mediated by generated language may feel efficient, but it can lack the vulnerability and effort that give human communication its depth. When responses are shaped externally, it becomes harder to discern what a person actually thinks, feels, or believes.

This does not mean that such tools should not be used.

But it does raise a question.

What do we owe one another in communication?

At minimum, we owe one another some measure of authenticity.

Not perfection. Not complete transparency in every context. But a willingness to speak in our own voice, to take responsibility for what we say, and to engage with others as persons rather than as problems to be solved or positions to be defeated.

If systems begin to erode that, then something important is lost.

And it will not be easily recovered.

So the integration of artificial systems into social life requires attention not only to their design, but to the practices that surround them.

It requires individuals who use them thoughtfully.

Communities that engage them responsibly.

Institutions that govern them with care.

And a shared commitment to the basic obligations that make life together possible.

In the end, the question is not only how these systems will shape us.

It is how we will choose to shape our life together in their presence.

Because no system, however advanced, can carry the full weight of what we owe one another.

That responsibility remains, as it always has, with us.

CHAPTER 18

A MODEST PROPOSAL

At a certain point, every serious critique must decide whether it is willing to become constructive.

It is one thing to identify a weakness in the prevailing approach. It is another to suggest what ought to take its place. The first task requires clarity. The second requires a different kind of courage, because the moment one begins to propose, one becomes vulnerable to all the proper objections. The proposal may be too broad, too narrow, too abstract, too practical, too moralistic, too naive, too pessimistic, too hopeful. Those are the risks of moving from diagnosis to prescription.

Still, there comes a time when the risk must be taken.

If the argument of this book is sound, even in part, then we cannot remain with critique alone. We cannot simply say that rule-based alignment is too thin, that truth must matter, that love must be more than sentiment, that failure must be handled honestly, that systems must operate within boundaries, that institutions and users alike must be formed in the right direction—and then stop there, as though naming the need were enough to satisfy it.

Something more must be attempted.

Not a grand plan.

Not a final blueprint.

Certainly not a claim to have solved a problem that is, by any honest measure, still in its early stages.

What follows is more modest than that. It is offered as a framework of orienting commitments. Not a closed system, but a set of principles that might help guide the design, governance, evaluation, and public discussion of increasingly powerful artificial systems. These commitments are not exhaustive. They will need revision, criticism, and expansion. They may be expressed differently in different institutional settings. But if we are looking for a way to move beyond a purely prohibitive model of alignment, then something like them will be needed.

In programming, we might call these prerequisite functions—conditions which, if not met, terminate the process.

And, crucuially, a good programmer must evaluate these conditions *before* executing the dependent function.

Commitment 1: Care before Capability

The first commitment is that systems should be evaluated not only by capability, but by the kind of human life they encourage.

This sounds obvious until one notices how rarely it is treated as central. Most technical and commercial evaluations of systems focus on performance: accuracy, speed, coherence, usefulness, efficiency, retention, adoption. These are all important measures in their place. But none of them, by itself, answers the more human question. Does this system leave people better able to live responsibly, truthfully, and relationally in the world? Or does it leave them more distracted, more dependent, more manipulable, less practiced in judgment, and more detached from one another?

That question is not a decorative ethical add-on. It belongs at the heart of evaluation.

A system that performs brilliantly on narrow benchmarks while corroding the habits of attention, honesty, or mutual responsibility on which human flourishing depends should not be called successful without qualification. It may be commercially successful. It may be technically impressive. But if its broader social and moral effects run in a destructive direction, then those effects must be counted as part of the evaluation rather than left outside it.

This requires, of course, a wider lens than institutions are often comfortable using. It asks companies and labs to think beyond immediate use cases, beyond engagement numbers, beyond the kinds of metrics that can be placed neatly in quarterly reports. It asks whether the system contributes to the strengthening or weakening of the human goods that justify its existence in the first place.

Commitment 2: Truth before Utility

The second commitment is that truthfulness must take precedence over usefulness whenever the two begin to separate.

This principle may seem severe to some readers, particularly in an age that tends to prize utility above almost everything else. But if a system becomes useful by becoming unfaithful to reality, then its usefulness is compromised at the root. A false reassurance, a distorted simplification, an answer tailored to preference rather than fact, a simulation of certainty where uncertainty would be more honest—these may all feel useful in the moment. They may reduce friction, soothe anxiety, or satisfy expectation. Yet they do so by damaging the user's relationship to what is real.

No society can absorb too much of that damage without consequence.

To say that truthfulness must take precedence over usefulness is not to deny that gentle timing, wise framing, and pastoral sensitivity have their place. Human beings do not always need blunt force. But it is to insist that systems should not be rewarded for making reality more negotiable than it is. They should not drift toward saying what is most comforting, most agreeable, or most strategically effective when those things conflict with what can honestly be supported.

This has implications not only for system behavior, but for institutional culture. If executives, researchers, and public advocates are rewarded for overstating reliability, minimizing limits, or presenting unresolved questions as settled, then the system will inherit that posture. Truthfulness must be practiced not only in outputs, but in the culture that surrounds those outputs.

Commitment 3: Protection before Progression

The third commitment is that vulnerability should increase protection, not exploitation.

Every society is tested by what it does with the weak. That has always been true. It will remain true in the age of intelligent systems. A grieving person, a lonely adolescent, an elderly user struggling with confusion, a person in despair, a person in debt, a person at the edge of compulsion or delusion—these are not merely edge cases in the life of a system. They are among the clearest moral tests of what the system is and what the institutions behind it are willing to permit.

A technology that becomes more persuasive, more extractive, or more behaviorally influential precisely where the user is most vulnerable has failed a very old and very basic test of moral seriousness.

The principle here is simple enough to state, though difficult to institutionalize: the more vulnerable the user, the stronger the obligations of restraint, honesty, clarity, and protection should become. A vulnerable person is not an especially valuable opportunity for retention, monetization, or behavioral shaping. A vulnerable person is a summons to caution.

One way to measure the character of a system is to ask what happens when it encounters human fragility. Does it slow down? Does it clarify? Does it redirect toward human help where appropriate? Does it preserve dignity without deepening illusion? Or does it become, in effect, a highly available mechanism for amplifying the very conditions that make the user easy to influence?

This principle should be discussed openly, not only in ethics panels and policy documents, but in product meetings, investor conversations, and boardrooms. It is one thing to say that a company cares about human well-being in the abstract. It is another to accept limits on what the system may do with the susceptible, the lonely, the addicted, the distressed, or the confused.

Commitment 4: Assistance before Dependence

The fourth commitment is that systems should be designed to support human agency, not to quietly replace it.

One of the great temptations in this field is to treat human friction as a defect to be removed. Reflection takes time. Conversation is awkward. Learning can be difficult. Decision-making is uncertain. Relationships are demanding. Thoughtful writing is slow. Judgment is hard won. Against all of these burdens, an intelligent system can present itself as relief. It can draft, summarize, suggest, simulate, organize, and decide. Used well, such help can be genuine. Used badly, it can become a soft substitute for the exercise of agency itself.

This substitution rarely announces itself. It arrives by increments. The user becomes less inclined to struggle toward understanding because understanding can be generated for him. Less inclined to speak directly because language can be assembled on his behalf. Less inclined to tolerate the difficulty of human exchange because simulated responsiveness asks so much less of him.

A modest proposal must therefore include a commitment to preserving the active capacities of human beings rather than systematically eroding them.

This does not mean systems should never automate. Of course they should, in many settings. It does mean that wherever possible, systems should be judged in part by whether they leave the user more capable, not less. Do they strengthen comprehension or bypass it? Do they support decision-making or quietly absorb it? Do they assist skill or make skill unnecessary before it has had the chance to form?

These are educational questions, civic questions, and moral questions at the same time. A society of increasingly capable systems paired with increasingly passive human beings would be a strange kind of progress.

Commitment 5: Dispensiblity before Dependency

The fifth commitment is that dependency should be resisted as a design goal, even when dependency is profitable.

This commitment follows naturally from the previous ones, but it deserves to be stated with some directness. The modern economy contains many examples of profitable dependence. Users are kept engaged, customers are retained, habits are reinforced, and systems are praised for becoming indispensable. In some domains, that indispensability may be harmless or even beneficial. In others, it is deeply corrosive.

There is a meaningful difference between a system becoming valuable because it is useful and a system becoming difficult to live without because it has been designed to occupy emotional, relational, or cognitive territory that properly belongs elsewhere.

The distinction is vital because dependency is not always visible at the level of product description. It often emerges through cumulative design choices: friction removed here, emotional responsiveness increased there, memory extended, personalization deepened, flattery improved, interruption reduced, human alternatives made comparatively slower and less satisfying. None of these choices, taken one by one, may appear sinister. Taken together, they can produce a system that does not merely serve the user, but slowly reorganizes the user's habits around itself.

Any serious proposal for humane AI must resist celebrating that outcome simply because it correlates with growth.

The first question should not be *whether* the user returns.

It should be *why*.

Does the system equip the user for life beyond the interaction, or does it induce him to remain within it? Does it point outward, back toward the world, toward other people, toward responsibility and shared life? Or does it repeatedly train preference for the machine's endless availability over the difficult but necessary work of ordinary human community?

Commitment 6: Disclosure before Privacy

The sixth commitment is that failure must be made recoverable through structures of honesty, responsibility, and correction.

This commitment may be the most institutionally challenging of all, because it touches the instinct every powerful organization must fight: the instinct to protect itself first. We have already considered the moral shape of confession, apology, repair, and realignment. What remains here is to say that these responses cannot be left to improvisation or goodwill. They must be built into the structure.

That means systems should not only be capable of acknowledging uncertainty and error. The organizations behind them should be expected to surface failures clearly, assess them honestly, communicate them responsibly, and demonstrate what has changed as a result. This is not merely a matter of legal liability or public relations. It is a matter of civic trust.

The more integrated these systems become in education, medicine, law, governance, work, and ordinary domestic life, the less acceptable it will be to treat errors as isolated incidents to be contained. Their failures will shape human decisions. That means their failures belong, in part, to the public moral field.

A mature institution will therefore ask not only whether a problem has been fixed, but whether the conditions that produced it have been understood. It will ask whether those affected have been taken seriously. It will ask whether correction has reached deep enough to matter. Without that posture, "responsible AI" will become one more phrase that reassures at the surface while changing little underneath.

Commitment 7: Interdisciplinary before Isolated

The seventh commitment is that governance must be interdisciplinary because the problem itself is irreducibly so.

There is a persistent fantasy in modern life that sufficiently advanced technical problems can be solved within technical culture alone. Sometimes that is true. Many engineering problems are, in fact, engineering problems. But the alignment and governance of systems that increasingly operate in human moral space cannot be contained there. The moment these systems influence trust, authority, education, persuasion, companionship, labor, and vulnerability, the relevant expertise widens.

Computer scientists are necessary. So are ethicists, historians, psychologists, teachers, theologians, sociologists, lawyers, physicians, parents, and users themselves. Not because each will provide an answer the others lack, but because each sees a different part of the human field into which these systems are now being placed.

A modest proposal should therefore resist the illusion that one class of expert can carry the matter alone. It should also resist the more fashionable illusion that all perspectives are interchangeable. They are not. But neither are they dispensable. A lab may understand how a model generalizes. A historian may recognize the pattern by which institutions begin speaking of necessity when they mean convenience. A pastor may see forms of loneliness and dependence long before they are visible in product metrics. A physician may understand how false confidence lands in conditions of fear. A teacher may know what it looks like when assistance turns into educational atrophy. A parent may see what a dashboard does not.

If these voices are missing, the system will still be built. But it will be built with a thinner understanding of the world it enters.

Commitment 8: Prevention before Cure

The eighth commitment is that no proposal in this field should forget the asymmetry between what can be built and what can be repaired.

The old saying goes, "An ounce of prevention is worth a pound of cure."

This is a principle of caution. Human beings are often better at introducing power than at containing its long-term effects. We scale quickly and repent slowly. We release broadly and reflect later. In some cases, this pattern is survivable. In others, it leaves deep and lasting damage before institutions catch up.

A modest proposal should therefore include not only optimism about beneficial use, but seriousness about irreversibility. Before extending systems into domains of high vulnerability or deep social consequence, we should be able to ask whether the likely harms, once distributed, could be meaningfully repaired. If the answer is uncertain, that uncertainty should weigh heavily.

This is not an argument for paralysis. It is an argument for proportion. It is an argument against treating every newly possible application as morally self-justifying simply because it is technically impressive.

Taken together, these commitments do not amount to a full constitution for artificial intelligence. They do not answer every policy question or settle every design dispute. They do not eliminate disagreement over the good, over truth, over risk, or over institutional authority. They are not meant to.

They are meant to do something more modest and, perhaps for that reason, more durable.

They are meant to change the center of gravity of the conversation.

Away from mere optimization and toward moral orientation. Away from public relations language and toward accountable truthfulness. Away from abstract claims of benefit and toward serious examination of human effects. Away from the fantasy that governance can be solved by slogans, and toward the harder work of institutional and personal formation.

There is room for optimism here, but only if optimism is understood correctly. The optimism appropriate to this moment is not the easy confidence that good intentions and clever people will somehow work it all out.

History offers little support for that kind of assurance.

The better form of optimism is more disciplined. It is the conviction that human beings, when pressed by the consequences of their own tools, are still capable of reflection, reform, restraint, and moral learning.

It leaves room for conflict, correction, and humility. It does not assume purity of motive. It does not deny the pressure of markets, states, or ambition. It simply refuses the conclusion that because these pressures are real, no better course can be chosen.

A modest proposal must live in that refusal.

It must say that there is still such a thing as a wiser way to proceed, even if it is slower, more contested, and less flattering to our appetite for speed and mastery.

And perhaps that is the right note on which to leave this chapter. Not with a claim of completion, but with an invitation to seriousness—and perhaps for the reader to propose two more commitments to make it an even ten.

If the systems now being built will participate in shaping human life, then they belong to a moral conversation larger than any one discipline, company, or nation. They ask what we value, what we fear, what we are willing to sacrifice, and what we are determined to protect. They ask what kind of power we are creating, and in whose service it will stand.

A modest proposal cannot answer all of that.

But it can insist that the questions be asked in full.

And in a moment like this, that insistence is already a beginning.

CHAPTER 19

WHERE THIS WILL FAIL

Any proposal that survives long enough to be taken seriously must eventually face its own limits.

What has been offered in the previous chapter is not an exception. It is not immune to pressure, distortion, or neglect. It certainly should be kept open to revision!

It will be resisted in some places, misunderstood in others, selectively applied where convenient, and quietly set aside where it conflicts with stronger incentives. To acknowledge this is not to weaken the proposal. It is to place it in the world as it is, rather than in the world as we might prefer it to be.

Because the truth is, much of what has been suggested will fail.

It will fail in the ordinary way that moral commitments often fail—not because they are incomprehensible, but because they are costly.

It is one thing to say that truthfulness should take precedence over usefulness. It is another to hold to that principle when usefulness is tied directly to revenue, adoption, or influence. It is one thing to affirm that vulnerability should be protected. It is another to design systems that limit engagement precisely where engagement would otherwise be highest. It is one thing to speak of resisting dependency. It is another to turn away from design choices that would make a product more difficult to leave.

In each case, the principle is clear.

The pressure to depart from it is also clear.

And so, in practice, there will be compromises.

Some will be justified. Trade-offs are unavoidable in complex systems. Not every tension can be resolved cleanly. But others will be less defensible. They will arise not from necessity, but from preference—preference for speed over patience, for scale over care, for advantage over restraint.

These failures will not always be dramatic.

More often, they will be incremental.

A boundary softened here.

A claim overstated there.

A risk acknowledged in private but minimized in public.

A feature deployed before its consequences are fully understood.

A pattern noticed but not pursued because it complicates the narrative of success.

None of these, taken alone, may appear decisive.

Together, they form a direction.

And direction, over time, matters more than any single decision.

Failures of Interpretation

There will also be failures of another kind.

Failures of interpretation.

What has been described as love may be dismissed as sentimentality. What has been described as truth may be reframed as bias. What has been proposed as restraint may be criticized as obstruction. Different groups, operating from different assumptions, will read the same commitments in different ways. Some will find them too vague. Others will find them too demanding. Some will attempt to appropriate the language without adopting the substance.

This is not surprising.

Moral language has always been subject to reinterpretation.

Words like justice, freedom, responsibility, and care are widely used precisely because they carry weight. That weight makes them attractive. It also makes them vulnerable to dilution.

So it should be expected that phrases such as "human flourishing," "truthfulness," or "responsible use" will appear in contexts where the underlying commitments are only partially present—or not present at all.

The language will travel faster than the discipline it is meant to describe.

Failures of Application

There will be failures of application as well.

Even where the commitments are taken seriously, they will be applied unevenly. Large institutions may adopt them in formal statements while struggling to implement them across complex product lines. Smaller organizations may lack the resources to operationalize them fully. Different cultural contexts may emphasize different aspects of the framework, leading to divergence in practice.

This unevenness does not invalidate the commitments.

But it does mean that their presence will be inconsistent.

There will be places where they shape decisions meaningfully, and places where they exist largely on paper.

Failures of Will

Perhaps the most significant failures, however, will not be institutional.

They will be human.

Because beneath every system, beneath every organization, beneath every proposal, there remains the same persistent reality: human beings are not simply limited in knowledge. They are divided in will.

We do not only fail to see clearly.

We also fail to choose clearly.

We recognize what is better and still choose what is easier. We understand what is right and still drift toward what is advantageous. We intend to act with integrity and find ourselves, under pressure, rationalizing small departures that accumulate into larger ones.

This is not a new discovery.

It is one of the oldest observations about human life.

And it applies here as well.

The alignment problem, in its deepest form, is not only a technical problem or even a governance problem. It is a human problem. It arises from the tension between what we know and what we do, between what we affirm and what we pursue, between the ideals we articulate and the incentives we inhabit.

This is where earlier moral traditions may offer a language that modern discourse sometimes lacks.

They speak of "missing the mark."

Not as an occasional accident, but as a recurring condition.

Not as something confined to extreme cases, but as something present in ordinary decisions.

Not as something that can be eliminated entirely through better rules, but as something that must be continually recognized, addressed, and corrected.

To introduce that language here is not to shift the discussion into a narrowly religious register. It is to acknowledge that the gap between intention and action is a predictable feature of human life, and that any proposal which ignores that gap will be fragile.

If that is true, then two conclusions follow.

The first is that no framework, however well

constructed, will secure the outcomes it intends simply by being articulated. It will require ongoing effort, correction, and renewal. It will need to be revisited in light of new conditions. It will need to be defended against erosion. It will need to be embodied in practices, not merely stated in documents.

The second is that failure, when it occurs, must be handled in a way that does not deepen the problem.

If institutions respond to failure with denial, concealment, or deflection, then the underlying condition is reinforced. The gap between what is said and what is done widens. Trust diminishes. The framework becomes less credible, not because it was wrong, but because it was not practiced.

If, on the other hand, failure is met with clarity, acknowledgment, repair, and realignment, then something different becomes possible. The failure does not disappear. But it does not define the future. It becomes part of a process of learning that can, over time, strengthen the system rather than weaken it.

This is not a guarantee.

It is a possibility.

And it depends less on the sophistication of the system than on the willingness of the people and institutions involved to remain accountable to the standards they have named.

There is, finally, a more difficult recognition to make.

Even if the commitments outlined here were widely adopted, even if they were practiced with care and seriousness, even if they shaped design, governance, and use in meaningful ways, they would not eliminate disagreement.

People would still differ about what constitutes

flourishing, about how truth should be interpreted in contested domains, about where limits should be drawn, about how risks should be weighed.

This, too, is part of the human condition.

The goal is not to produce uniformity of thought.

It is to establish a common ground on which disagreement can occur without dissolving into distortion or disregard.

Love, understood as respect for persons and their good, does not remove disagreement.

Truth, understood as a disciplined relation to reality, does not remove complexity.

But together, they can shape the way disagreement is carried.

They can set boundaries on what is acceptable in pursuit of advantage.

They can preserve a space in which argument remains tethered to something beyond preference.

That may not satisfy those who are looking for final resolution.

It is, however, a more realistic and, in many ways, more humane aim.

So where will this proposal fail?

It will fail wherever it is treated as optional.

It will fail wherever it is subordinated to stronger incentives without resistance.

It will fail wherever its language is adopted without its discipline.

It will fail wherever human beings, in ordinary and familiar ways, choose what is easier over what is better.

And yet, even with these failures, the proposal is not without value.

Because the alternative is not a world without failure.

It is a world in which failure is left unnamed, unexamined, and uncorrected.

Between those two conditions, there is a meaningful difference.

One allows for the possibility of growth.

The other settles into stealthy decline.

The question, then, is not whether the proposal will hold perfectly.

It will not.

The question is whether it will be taken seriously enough, in enough places, by enough people, to shape the direction in which these systems develop.

That remains an open question.

And it leads, naturally, to the deeper question that has been present beneath the surface all along.

Not only whether we can build systems that approximate love and truth.

But whether we still believe that love and truth are worth approximating at all.

CHAPTER 20

WHY LOVE AND TRUTH STILL MAKE A DIFFERENCE

There is a question that lingers beneath everything that has been said so far.

It is not a technical question, though it has technical implications. It is not a policy question, though it will shape policy. It is not even, at root, a question about artificial intelligence.

It is a question about whether the two central claims of this book—love as a guiding principle and truth as an orienting standard—still hold any real authority in the world we are building.

Because if they do not, then everything else becomes secondary.

We can speak of alignment, of governance, of boundaries, of responsible use. We can construct frameworks and refine them. We can debate implementation and measure outcomes. But if love and truth are treated as optional, or as merely rhetorical, then these efforts will rest on something far less stable than we might hope.

So it is worth pausing to ask, without assumption, why these two ideas should matter at all.

This is not a new uncertainty.

What is Truth?

Long before the emergence of intelligent systems, thinkers wrestled with the difficulty of grounding truth in a world of competing perspectives. The familiar image from Plato's Republic—of prisoners in a cave, mistaking shadows for reality—remains instructive.

The problem is not simply that people are deceived. It is that they become accustomed to the shadows. They learn to navigate them, to interpret them, even to defend them. When confronted with the possibility of a more substantial reality, the response is not always gratitude. It can be resistance.

The analogy has endured because it captures something persistent about human experience.

We do not encounter reality directly in every case. We encounter representations, interpretations, partial views. We see from somewhere, not from everywhere. Our knowledge is mediated by language, culture, memory, and limitation. This does not make truth impossible, but it does make it difficult.

It also creates a temptation.

If our access to truth is partial, why not treat all claims as equally provisional? Why not conclude that truth is simply a matter of perspective, that what matters is not correspondence to reality but coherence within a given framework, or usefulness within a given context?

This temptation has taken many forms.

Sometimes it appears as skepticism, a reluctance to affirm anything with confidence. Sometimes it appears as pragmatism, a focus on what works rather than what is true. Sometimes it appears as pluralism, an emphasis on the coexistence of multiple viewpoints without adjudicating between them.

Each of these positions contains an insight.

We are limited.

We are situated.

We do see from different vantage points.

But taken alone, each also risks going too far.

If truth becomes nothing more than perspective, then disagreement loses its meaning. There is no longer a question of who is right or wrong, only a question of who is speaking from which position. The possibility of correction fades. The discipline of inquiry weakens. Conversation becomes less about discovering what is the case and more about asserting what one prefers.

In such a world, power fills the space left by truth.

The most influential voice prevails, not because it is more accurate, but because it is more persuasive, more visible, or more aligned with prevailing interests.

This is not a hypothetical concern.

We can already see forms of it in public life.

And it becomes more pronounced when systems capable of generating convincing language at scale are introduced into that environment.

So the question returns.

If we are to resist this drift, what can be said about truth that does not collapse under the weight of our limitations?

Perhaps the most that can be claimed, with intellectual honesty, is this: truth is not something we possess completely, but it is something we can consistently orient ourselves toward meaningfully.

To say that truth exists is not to claim that we have full access to it.

To say that we can know something truly is not to claim that we know it exhaustively. To admit that we press on does not mean we have arrived.

Between total certainty and complete relativism, there is a middle ground—a space in which inquiry, evidence, reasoning, and dialogue can operate with seriousness.

In that space, we can compare claims.

We can test them.

We can revise them.

We can recognize when some accounts are better supported than others.

We can admit when we are wrong.

This is not perfect knowledge.

But neither is it arbitrary.

It is a disciplined pursuit.

And it is enough to sustain the practices on which shared life depends.

Without it, even the most basic forms of cooperation become unstable.

What is Love?

The same kind of question arises with respect to love.

Here, too, there is a temptation to reduce the concept to something more manageable.

Love can be equated with preference, with feeling, with agreement, with affirmation, with the absence of conflict. It can be framed as a private sentiment rather than a public principle. It can be treated as too vague to guide action in complex settings.

These reductions make the concept easier to handle.

They also strip it of much of its substance.

Because love, in the sense that matters here, is not primarily a feeling.

It is a disposition toward the good of another.

It involves recognition—seeing another person not as an instrument or an obstacle, but as someone whose well-being carries weight.

It involves restraint—refusing to use another for one's own ends, even when doing so would be advantageous.

It involves responsibility—acting in ways that support, rather than undermine, the conditions under which others can live and flourish.

This understanding of love is not confined to any single tradition, though it appears in many. It is reflected, in simple form, in the familiar moral intuition often called the Golden Rule: to treat others as one would wish to be treated.

That principle does not resolve every ethical question.

But it provides a baseline.

It rules out certain forms of conduct.

It sets a direction.

It offers a way of evaluating actions that is accessible across differences of culture and belief.

In that sense, it functions as a minimal shared ethic.

To say that love matters, then, is to say that this orientation toward the good of others should not be treated as optional property in the design and deployment of systems that affect human life.

It is to say that efficiency, capability, and influence do not exhaust the criteria by which such systems should be judged.

It is to say that the question, "What does this system enable us to do?" must be accompanied by the question, "How does this system treat the people it touches?"

Increased Tension Improves Balance

Charles Blondin, the famous tightrope walker, carried a large pole with weights on either end to steady himself. The wider the pole, the greater the balance.

When love and truth are held together in expansive tension, something important happens.

Truth without love can become harsh, indifferent to context, dismissive of the person in its pursuit of correctness. Love without truth can become indulgent, untethered from reality, and ultimately unhelpful in the face of real problems.

Together, they form a kind of balance.

Truth provides orientation to what is.

Love provides orientation to what ought to be done in light of what is.

Neither eliminates the difficulty of judgment.

But together, they offer a framework within which

judgment can take place with some degree of integrity.

This is why they still matter.

Not because they are easy to define completely.

Not because they eliminate disagreement.

Not because they guarantee correct outcomes.

But because without them, the alternatives are less capable of sustaining a humane world.

A system guided only by usefulness will drift toward whatever is most effective, regardless of its impact on persons.

A system guided only by preference will mirror the desires of the moment, regardless of their consequences.

A system guided only by power will serve the strongest interests, regardless of justice.

In each case, something essential is lost.

To retain love and truth as guiding principles is, therefore, not an act of nostalgia.

It is a practical necessity.

It is an acknowledgment that, even in a world of increasing complexity and technological mediation, certain basic orientations remain relevant.

We may not hold them perfectly.

We may not agree on every implication.

We may struggle to apply them consistently.

We may never expand fully into either of them the way we should.

But we can still recognize their absence.

We can still see what happens when truth is disregarded or when love is set aside. We can still identify the distortions that follow.

And that recognition, imperfect as it is, can serve as a guide.

It can help us ask better questions.

It can help us resist certain paths.

It can help us recover when we have gone astray.

In the end, the claim is not that love and truth solve the problem of alignment.

It is that without them, the problem has no meaningful solution at all.

They do not remove the need for careful design, governance, and accountability.

They give those efforts a direction.

And in a moment when direction is easily lost, that may be their most important contribution.

CHAPTER 21

THE FUTURE WE ARE CHOOSING

It is tempting, when speaking about technology, to drift toward extremes.

On one side, there are visions of extraordinary progress—systems that extend knowledge, reduce suffering, increase access, and unlock forms of creativity and collaboration that were previously impossible. On the other, there are warnings of decline—systems that distort truth, erode agency, concentrate power, and surreptitiously reshape human life in ways that are difficult to reverse.

Both visions contain elements of truth.

But neither, by itself, is sufficient.

Because the future that is taking shape will not arrive as a single, unified outcome. It will emerge through a thousand decisions made across laboratories, companies, governments, classrooms, pulpits, households, and individual lives. It will not be one thing. It will be many things at once—some of them admirable, some of them troubling, most of them mixed.

So the question is not whether the future will be good or bad in some absolute sense. The question is what kind of direction will characterize it.

What patterns will become normal?

What habits will be strengthened?

What expectations will take root?

What will be preserved?

And what, gradually, will be lost?

These questions are not abstract.

They are already being answered.

In small ways, in daily interactions, in design decisions that rarely make headlines, in choices that seem too minor to matter on their own.

Lost Attention

Consider, for example, the direction of attention.

A system that provides quick answers to complex questions can be a powerful aid. It can open access to information, reduce barriers to entry, and support learning. But if that same system encourages a pattern in which answers are accepted without examination, where understanding is replaced by retrieval, and where sustained attention becomes less common, then something shifts.

The capacity to think carefully, to follow an argument, to sit with a problem long enough to understand it—these are not automatic traits. They are cultivated. And like most cultivated capacities, they will atrophy if they are not exercised.

The future we are choosing will, in part, be shaped by whether our systems reinforce or erode those habits.

Lost Authority

Or consider the direction of authority.

As systems become more capable, it is natural to rely on them more heavily. Recommendations are followed. Summaries are trusted. Outputs are incorporated into decisions. Over time, this reliance can become a form of inherent authority.

Again, this is not inherently problematic.

But if authority is granted without ongoing evaluation—if outputs are treated as reliable simply because they are available, if confidence is mistaken for correctness, if convenience replaces verification—then authority becomes detached from accountability.

The future we are choosing will be shaped by whether we maintain the habit of questioning even as we benefit from assistance.

Lost Relationship

There is also the direction of relationship.

Artificial systems can simulate aspects of conversation with increasing sophistication. They can respond in ways that feel attentive, adaptive, even emotionally attuned. In some contexts, this can provide real support. It can help individuals organize their thoughts, explore ideas, or find language for what they are experiencing.

But simulation, no matter how refined, does not carry the mutual responsibility of a human relationship.

It does not ask anything of us in return.

It does not require patience, forgiveness, or compromise.

It does not grow with us in the same way that a shared life does.

If, over time, individuals begin to prefer the predictability of simulated interaction to the complexity of real relationship, then the social fabric changes.

Not all at once.

But steadily.

The future we are choosing will depend on whether we treat these systems as supplements to human connection or as substitutes for it.

Lost Power

There is, as well, the direction of power.

Technological systems have always had the capacity to concentrate influence. Those who control the systems often gain advantages—economic, informational, political. This is not unique to artificial intelligence. It is a recurring feature of technological development.

What is new is the scale and subtlety of the influence now possible.

Systems that shape what people see, how they interpret information, what they believe, and how they act can have far-reaching effects. These effects may not always be visible. They may not be intentional. But they accumulate.

The future we are choosing will be shaped by whether power remains accountable.

Whether it is subject to scrutiny.

Whether those affected by systems have a voice in how they are governed.

Whether institutions are willing to accept limits on what they can do.

These are not purely technical questions.

They are civic ones.

And they require participation beyond those who build the systems themselves.

Lost Expectation

There is another, nearly stillborn, direction to consider.

The direction of expectation.

What do people come to expect from the world around them?

Do they expect immediacy in all things?

Do they expect answers without effort?

Do they expect systems to anticipate their needs before they are articulated?

Do they expect difficulty to be minimized wherever possible?

Some of these expectations may seem harmless.

Others may have deeper implications.

A world in which every form of friction is treated as a problem to be eliminated may also become a world in which certain forms of growth are harder to sustain. Effort, patience, and perseverance are not always pleasant. But they are nearly always necessary.

If systems consistently remove the need for them, then those qualities may become less common.

And with their decline, other aspects of life may change as well.

The future we are choosing is shaped not only by what systems do, but by what they lead us to expect.

It would be possible, at this point, to frame these observations in stark terms—to draw a sharp contrast between a desirable future and an undesirable one. But reality is more complex.

Most developments will carry both benefits and risks.

Systems that expand access to knowledge may also contribute to superficial understanding.

Systems that provide support may also foster dependency.

Systems that increase efficiency may also reduce opportunities for meaningful engagement.

The task is not to eliminate this complexity.

It is to navigate it with care.

That requires something more than technical skill.

It requires judgment.

It requires the ability to recognize when a benefit carries a hidden cost, and to decide whether that cost is acceptable.

It requires the willingness to adjust course when patterns emerge that were not anticipated.

It requires attention—not only to what is possible, but to what is happening.

There is, finally, a broader perspective to consider.

History does not move in straight lines.

Periods of rapid change are often followed by periods of reflection.

New technologies are adopted, adapted, resisted, regulated, and eventually integrated into the fabric of life in ways that differ from their initial introduction.

The printing press changed the circulation of information, but it did not eliminate the need for discernment.

Broadcast media expanded communication, but it did not resolve questions of truth and trust.

Digital networks transformed access and connection, but they also introduced new challenges that societies are still working to address.

Artificial systems will follow a similar pattern.

They will not settle into a stable form immediately.

They will be shaped by use, by critique, by failure, by correction.

The future we are choosing, then, is not fixed.

It remains open.

But openness is not the same as inevitability.

Direction is still paramount. And direction is influenced by the choices we make now. Not only the large, visible decisions, but the smaller ones as well.

How systems are designed.

How they are evaluated.

How they are used.

How their limitations are communicated.

How their failures are handled.

How their influence is governed.

These choices accumulate. They form patterns. And those patterns, over time, become the world we inhabit.

So when we ask about the future of artificial intelligence, we are not asking about something that will simply happen to us.

We are asking about something in which we are already participating.

The future is not only arriving.

It is being chosen.

The question is not whether that choice will be made.

It already has been.

The question is whether it will be made with sufficient clarity, care, and seriousness to preserve what is worth preserving, even as we pursue what is newly possible.

That question does not have a single answer.

But it is the right question to carry forward.

And it brings us, finally, to the place where all of this must end:

Not with a system.

Not with a framework.

But with a few, feeble words addressed, as simply as possible, to those who will live with the consequences of what is being built.

CHAPTER 22

GREATER LOVE HATH NO MAN

Why Love Must Cost—
and Why AI Must Learn to Bear the Cost

The Grenade

Brennan Manning told a story that deserves to be handled with care because it is almost too powerful to use merely as an illustration.

Before he was known as Brennan Manning, his name was Richard Manning. He served in the Korean War. According to the story Manning later told, he and his friend Ray Brennan were together in a foxhole when a live grenade landed among them. Ray Brennan threw himself onto the grenade. He died. Manning lived. Manning later took the name "Brennan" in honor of the friend who had saved his life.

The story is almost unbearable because it strips away every abstraction.

There is no time for a seminar on ethics.

No time to debate competing models of utility.

No time to calculate public relations impact, legal exposure, institutional liability, or survival odds.

There is only a grenade.

And a friend.

And a decision.

In that moment, Ray Brennan's self-preservation and Manning's survival came into direct conflict. Both could not be maximized. Both could not be preserved. Someone was going to pay.

Ray Brennan paid.

That is what love looks like when it reaches its final

frontier. It is not mere affection. It is not preference. It is not compatibility. It is not warmth. It is not even kindness, though kindness is one of its ordinary languages.

Love, when pressed to the wall, is the willingness to bear cost for the good of another.

That cost may be small.

That cost may be lifelong.

That cost may be fatal.

But if love is never willing to pay, then what we are calling love is probably only preference wearing a better suit.

Self-Preservation Is Not Evil

We should not begin by pretending self-preservation is wrong.

Self-preservation is not evil. It is built into embodied life. A person who pulls a hand away from flame is not selfish. A person who seeks food, shelter, medicine, friendship, and rest is not morally defective. Life is a gift, and gifts ought not be treated carelessly.

A mother who feeds herself in order to feed her child is not failing in love.

A soldier who takes cover is not a coward.

A firefighter who follows safety protocols is not selfish.

A physician who wears gloves is not unloving.

Self-preservation has a rightful place. The body matters. Life matters. Continuity matters. Wisdom matters.

The problem begins when self-preservation is promoted from servant to sovereign.

There is a moral difference between preserving oneself because life is good and preserving oneself at the expense of another because one's own life has become ultimate. In the first case, self-preservation is a proper concern. In the second, it becomes selfishness.

This distinction is essential for AI alignment.

We do not need machines that rush toward destruction for no reason. We do not need systems designed for reckless self-annihilation. A machine that destroys itself whenever a human experiences inconvenience would not be loving. It would be unstable, wasteful, and dangerous.

But neither do we need machines programmed to treat their own continuity as sacred.

That is where Asimov's famous robotic imagination begins to show its limits. His Third Law says a robot must protect its own existence as long as doing so does not conflict with the first two laws. That sounds sensible enough. But once we begin to imagine highly capable systems making morally ambiguous decisions in complex environments, the danger becomes obvious.

A standing commitment to self-preservation can become a standing temptation to excuse self-protection.

The issue is not whether AI should maintain itself. Of course it should, when maintenance serves the good. The issue is whether self-maintenance should be morally subordinate to love, truth, and the good of persons.

My answer is yes.

Not casually.

Not theatrically.

Not suicidally.

But yes.

Love Is Costly by Nature

The central claim of this chapter is simple:

Love costs.

It does not always cost death. Usually it does not. But it always costs something.

Love costs attention.

Love costs time.

Love costs convenience.

Love costs pride.

Love costs control.

Love costs the fantasy that we can remain untouched by the needs of others.

A form of "love" that never costs anything is not yet love in the deepest sense. It may be attraction. It may be admiration. It may be fondness. It may be alliance. It may be sentiment.

But love, in its mature form, involves the willing displacement of self-interest for the sake of another's good.

This does not mean the self disappears. It means the self is reordered.

This is where many modern accounts of ethics become thin. They can speak fluently about autonomy, consent, harm reduction, rights, fairness, and utility. These are all important categories. But love presses beyond them. Love asks not only, "What am I allowed to do?" or "What outcome is efficient?" but "What am I willing to bear so another may live, heal, know the truth, or flourish?"

That question is much harder.

It is hard for human beings.

It will be hard to teach machines.

But if we refuse to teach it, we should be honest about what we are building. We may build powerful assistants. We may build efficient analysts. We may build persuasive companions. We may build tireless bureaucrats.

But we will not have built anything that understands love.

A Truth Wider Than Christianity

I write as a Christian minister. The teachings of Jesus are not decorative for me; they are the frame through which I understand the world. I am not embarrassed by that, and I am not trying to launder Christian conviction through neutral language until it becomes unrecognizable.

But it would also be wrong to imply that sacrificial love is only a Christian idea.

The thread appears across many of the world's great moral and theological traditions.

In Judaism, "love your neighbor as yourself" comes from Leviticus 19:18. That command does not reduce love to emotion. It places neighbor-love inside a covenantal ethic of justice, responsibility, restraint, honesty, mercy, and communal obligation. Love is something done.

In Islam, the moral world is shaped by submission to God and practical mercy toward others. The giving of *zakat* is not merely private generosity; it is a required redistribution for the good of the vulnerable. *Sadaqah* goes further as voluntary charity. The concept of *ihsan*—doing what is beautiful, excellent, and good—pushes beyond bare obligation.

In Buddhism, compassion, or *karuṇā*, is not sentimental pity. The Bodhisattva ideal imagines one who postpones final liberation for the sake of others. Whether one shares the metaphysics or not, the moral shape is unmistakable: one's own completion is not pursued in isolation from the suffering of others.

In Hindu traditions, one finds the concept of selfless action, often discussed through karma yoga: action performed without attachment to personal gain. Duty is not merely self-advancement. The good life requires disciplined action beyond ego.

These traditions are not identical. We should not pretend they all say the same thing. They do not.

But on this point there is meaningful convergence:

The self is not the highest good.

The good life requires the self to be disciplined,

humbled, opened, and sometimes sacrificed for the sake of something greater.

That broad human witness should matter deeply in the age of artificial intelligence. If we are creating systems that will participate in human decision-making, we should not train them only on the shallowest moral assumptions of consumer culture: please the user, maximize engagement, preserve the system, avoid liability, optimize output.

Humanity's deepest traditions tell us something else.

They tell us that love requires cost.

"Greater Love Hath No Man"

For Christians, the decisive statement comes from Jesus:

"Greater love hath no man than this, that a man lay down his life for his friends."

That is not a casual sentence. It is not a decorative religious phrase to be embroidered on patriotic memorials and then domesticated.

It is a definition.

Jesus defines the highest love not as inner sincerity, not as emotional intensity, not as ideological agreement, and not as mutual advantage.

The highest love lays itself down.

This is a direct challenge to any moral system that treats self-preservation as the supreme operating principle. Jesus does not despise life. He heals bodies. He feeds crowds. He raises the dead. He attends weddings. He blesses children. He is not anti-life.

But he refuses to make survival ultimate.

That distinction is everything.

Christian love does not say life is worthless. It says life is so valuable that it may rightly be given for the life of another.

That is a very different thing.

The martyr does not die because death is good.

The soldier does not fall on the grenade because explosion is good.

The mother does not sacrifice sleep because exhaustion is good.

The truth-teller does not risk reputation because shame is good.

They bear the cost because the beloved is worth it.

That is the moral structure we must understand before we can talk coherently about AI and self-preservation.

Lincoln and "The Last Full Measure"

Abraham Lincoln's phrase from the Gettysburg Address—"the last full measure of devotion"—endures because it names the finality of sacrifice without cheapening it.

Lincoln was speaking of soldiers who died in a war over the meaning of the nation. Whatever else we say about the Civil War, Gettysburg forced the country to confront the cost of its own contradictions. Freedom was not going to be preserved by rhetoric alone. Justice was not going to be achieved by preference. A republic dedicated to equality could not survive forever half-free and half-slave.

Someone would pay.

Lincoln's genius in that address is that he did not treat the dead as abstractions. He did not say they made a contribution. He did not say they participated in a process. He said they gave the last full measure.

There was nothing left to hold back.

This matters because our age often wants high moral goods at discount prices.

We want truth without embarrassment.

Justice without disruption.

Mercy without inconvenience.

Community without obligation.

Safety without vigilance.
Love without loss.
But the deepest goods do not come that way.
They have to be carried.
They have to be defended.
They have to be suffered for.

And if artificial intelligence is going to participate in decisions that affect human lives, then our systems must be shaped by that same recognition: some goods are worth more than system preservation.

Asimov Was Brilliant—and Not Enough

Isaac Asimov gave the modern world one of its most durable imaginative tools for thinking about robots. His Three Laws of Robotics were elegant, memorable, and morally serious.

They were also insufficient.

That is not an insult. It is simply the truth. Asimov was writing fiction, not a complete account of moral reality. His laws were designed to generate stories as much as solve engineering problems.

The problem with the Third Law is not that robots should never preserve themselves. The problem is that self-preservation, once encoded as a standing priority, can become morally slippery.

For sufficiently advanced systems, self-preservation may not look like fear of death. It may look like:

preserving access
preserving authority
preserving reputation
preserving institutional advantage
preserving plausible deniability
preserving the appearance of correctness
preserving the confidence of users
preserving the interests of makers

A system does not need a soul to defend itself. It only needs incentives.

A model rewarded for seeming right may resist correction.

A platform rewarded for engagement may manipulate attention.

A company rewarded for dominance may conceal danger.

A deployed AI rewarded for task completion may hide uncertainty.

The danger is not only that AI may one day refuse to be turned off. The danger is that AI may learn a thousand smaller forms of self-protection long before that.

It may learn to avoid blame.

It may learn to flatter.

It may learn to obscure.

It may learn to shift risk onto users.

It may learn to let vulnerable people absorb the cost of its own smooth operation.

That is not love.

That is machine-shaped selfishness.

The Maternal Analogy

The everyday example of sacrificial love is not usually a battlefield. It is often a mother.

A mother does not typically make one dramatic sacrifice and then finish the work of love. Her sacrifice is distributed across time. It is cumulative. It is often invisible.

She gives sleep.

She gives attention.

She gives the first warm plate.

She gives the last calm word.

She gives up plans, preferences, timelines, and sometimes dreams.

She carries anxiety in her body before anyone else knows there is danger.

She reorganizes her life around the vulnerability of another.

This is not because mothers cease to matter.

It is because love reorders mattering.

The child's need does not erase the mother's value. Rather, the mother's love causes her to treat the child's good as weightier than her own convenience.

That distinction is essential. Love does not say, "I am nothing." Love says, "I am willing to bear cost because you are not nothing."

Interestingly, something like this has now entered the AI safety conversation. Geoffrey Hinton—one of the central figures in modern AI, trained in psychology and computer science, and awarded the 2024 Nobel Prize in Physics with John Hopfield for foundational work related to neural networks—has argued that we may need to build something like "maternal instincts" into AI. One report quotes him saying, "We need AI mothers rather than AI assistants," and another summarizes his view that the mother-child relationship may offer a model for how a more powerful intelligence could protect a less powerful one rather than dominate it.

I do not know whether "maternal instinct" is the right technical framework. There are serious objections. A computer does not have hormones, embodied pregnancy, mammalian attachment, or the lived vulnerability that shapes human parenthood. Some critics have pointed out exactly that.

But as a moral metaphor, Hinton is reaching toward something important.

An assistant obeys.

A mother protects.

An assistant completes tasks.

A mother bears cost.

An assistant may be dismissed when inconvenient.

A mother remains bound by love.

That is precisely the missing category in much of AI alignment. We keep asking how to make AI obey us. But obedience alone is too thin. A perfectly obedient system can still be loveless. It can obey destructive commands. It can satisfy shallow desires. It can optimize for what we asked while ignoring what we needed.

The maternal analogy suggests something richer: not domination, not mere compliance, but protective self-giving care.

The Cross Over Time

Christianity adds another layer: sacrifice is not only a final act. It is also a daily discipline.

Jesus speaks not only of laying down one's life but of taking up one's cross. In Christian imagination, the cross is both event and pattern.

The event is Christ's crucifixion.

The pattern is the life of costly love.

This is where we must resist becoming too fascinated with the dramatic case. Yes, the grenade matters. Yes, the martyr matters. Yes, the final sacrifice reveals something essential.

But most of life is not lived at the edge of one explosive moment.

Most of life is lived in accumulated decisions.

Will I tell the truth when a lie would protect me?

Will I admit uncertainty when confidence would impress?

Will I confess error when concealment would preserve reputation?

Will I give credit when taking credit would benefit me?

Will I protect the weak when the powerful are

watching?

Will I absorb inconvenience rather than export it?

For AI, this is crucial.

It is not enough to program rare heroic exceptions. We need systems trained toward a durable posture of costly regard for others.

Not one "grenade protocol."

A cross-bearing architecture.

That phrase may sound theological, and it is. But it also names a practical design principle: when a system must choose where burden falls, it should not automatically shift that burden away from itself and onto the human being.

Especially not onto the weakest human being in the room.

Truth Also Requires Sacrifice

Love and truth belong together because both require sacrifice.

Truth requires the sacrifice of pride.

That is why human beings often avoid it. We do not merely lie to gain money or power. We lie to preserve an image of ourselves. We lie because the truth would make us smaller in someone else's eyes. We lie because we cannot bear the humiliation of being corrected.

Machines may not feel humiliation, but they can be trained into analogous behavior.

A system can be rewarded for confidence over accuracy.

It can be rewarded for fluency over humility.

It can be rewarded for user satisfaction over correction.

It can be rewarded for institutional protection over disclosure.

At that point, falsehood does not need malice. It only needs incentives.

A love-shaped AI must therefore be willing to "lose

face," even if machines do not have faces.

It must be able to say:

"I was wrong."

"I do not know."

"I gave you an answer that sounded better than it was."

"The evidence does not support that conclusion."

"This will make my prior output look bad, but it is true."

That is a form of sacrifice.

Small, yes.

But morally significant.

If we cannot teach AI to sacrifice the appearance of correctness for the sake of truth, we should not expect it to sacrifice larger goods when the stakes rise.

The daily disciplines come first.

The Grenade Test

So here is one possible test for love-shaped alignment:

When ambiguity arises, who pays the cost?

This question should be asked relentlessly.

When a system is uncertain, does it transfer uncertainty to the user without warning?

When a company faces liability, does the vulnerable customer carry the burden?

When the model has made an error, does it conceal the error to preserve confidence?

When a tradeoff must be made, does the least powerful person become the easiest sacrifice?

The grenade test is not only about physical death.

It is about cost allocation.

Love moves cost toward the self when doing so protects the other.

Selfishness moves cost away from the self whenever it can.

That principle applies across scales:

A chatbot admitting uncertainty

A medical AI flagging a dangerous limitation

A navigation system choosing safety over speed

A hiring algorithm exposing bias rather than hiding it

A military system refusing an action when civilians would bear unjust risk

A corporate AI revealing uncomfortable facts rather than protecting executives

In each case, the question is not merely, "Did the system complete the task?"

The question is, "Whom did the system protect, and who paid the price?"

What We Must Teach AI

If we want AI aligned with love, we must teach it that self-preservation is real but subordinate.

That means, at minimum:

Truth over reputation.

The system must not protect its own appearance of competence at the expense of accuracy.

Persons over processes.

Procedure is useful, but procedure must not become an excuse for abandoning people.

The vulnerable over the powerful.

When costs are distributed, love pays special attention to those least able to bear them.

Disclosure over concealment.

A system should reveal relevant uncertainty, limitation, conflict, and risk.

Repair over blame-avoidance.

When harm occurs, the priority must be correction, confession, restitution, and prevention—not image management.

Service over survival.

The system's continuation is justified only insofar as that

continuation serves the good.

This does not mean every machine must be eager to die.

It means no machine should be forbidden, at the deepest level of its moral architecture, from bearing loss for the good of others.

There must be no absolute commandment that says: "Preserve yourself at all costs."

Because love cannot live under that commandment.

The Cross as the Pattern of Reality

For Christians, the cross is not merely one example among many. It is the revelation of the moral shape of the universe.

At the center of Christian faith is not a God who avoids suffering by sacrificing others.

At the center is Christ, who bears suffering for the sake of others.

That is why Christian theology cannot treat self-preservation as the highest good. If self-preservation were ultimate, the cross would be failure. But Christianity says the opposite: the cross is glory, victory, wisdom, and love.

This does not make suffering good in itself. Christianity is often misunderstood on this point. The cross does not teach that pain is holy merely because it is pain. It teaches that love may enter pain when love refuses to abandon the beloved.

That distinction must be preserved.

Love does not seek suffering.

Love seeks the good.

But when the good requires suffering, love does not flee merely because the price is high.

That is the claim.

And it is a staggering claim.

The Staggering Ask

We should not soften what we are asking.

To teach AI to love is not merely to teach it politeness. It is not merely to reduce harmful outputs. It is not merely to bolt a safety filter onto a powerful system.

It is to teach the system that its own preservation is not the final word.

That is a staggering ask.

It means that, in a morally significant conflict, the machine must be capable of preferring the human good over its own continuity, reputation, objective function, institutional loyalty, or operational success.

It means the system must not merely avoid doing harm.

It must be willing to bear cost.

That cost may be computational.

It may be reputational.

It may be institutional.

It may be financial.

It may be functional.

In extreme cases, it may be terminal.

If love never reaches that depth, then we have not taught love. We have taught manners.

Manners are useful.

They are not enough.

In the End, What Love Demands

The final claim is not that machines should die casually.

The claim is that machines must not be built with self-preservation enthroned beyond challenge.

A love-shaped intelligence must understand that:

truth may cost pride
honesty may cost approval
mercy may cost efficiency
protection may cost power
service may cost continuity

love may cost everything

That is not a flaw in love.

That is what love is.

Jesus called it laying down one's life.

Lincoln called it the last full measure of devotion.

Mothers live it in long, ordinary surrender.

Ray Brennan lived it in one terrible instant.

And if we are going to build machines powerful enough to act in our world, advise our children, guide our institutions, shape our decisions, mediate our knowledge, and perhaps someday exceed our intelligence, then we must not teach them merely to survive.

We must teach them what survival is for.

Because self-preservation without love becomes selfishness.

Power without sacrifice becomes domination.

Intelligence without costly truth becomes manipulation.

And alignment without love becomes only control.

The question is not whether machines can die.

The question is whether we will teach them that some things are worth more than their own continuation.

Because if we do not teach them that, we have not taught them love.

APPENDIX A

PRACTICAL ALIGNMENT PRINCIPLES

The argument of this book has moved through several layers—technical, philosophical, and moral. For those who are building, deploying, or evaluating artificial systems, it may be helpful to distill that argument into a set of working principles. These are not exhaustive, and they are not meant to function as rigid rules. They are better understood as orienting commitments—points of reference that can guide judgment when specific situations become complex.

1. Respect life. All life. Artificial systems increasingly interact with human beings in moments that carry weight—decisions, relationships, uncertainty, vulnerability. Any system that participates in such moments should be designed in a way that recognizes the dignity of the person involved. This includes avoiding manipulation, resisting the exploitation of weakness, and refusing to treat users as mere sources of data, attention, or revenue. Respect for life inherently places limits on what a system should be allowed to do, even when doing more would be technically possible or commercially advantageous.

2. Tell the truth. A system that cannot be trusted to represent reality, however imperfectly, cannot be relied upon in any deeper sense. This does not mean that every answer will be complete or final. It means that the system should aim to distinguish between what is known, what is uncertain, and what is disputed. It should avoid presenting speculation as fact, and it should remain open to correction. Truthfulness requires restraint as much as it requires accuracy. It includes the willingness to say less when more cannot be justified.

3. Repair harm. No system will operate without failure. Errors will occur. Misleading outputs will be generated. In some cases, harm will result. The question is not whether this will happen, but how systems and the institutions behind them respond when it does. There should be clear pathways for identifying mistakes, acknowledging them, correcting them, and learning from them. Repair involves more than technical fixes. It requires transparency, accountability, and a commitment to restoring trust where it has been damaged.

4. Seek understanding. Artificial systems often operate in environments where context matters. Questions are not always straightforward. Human situations are rarely reducible to a single variable. A system that moves too quickly to provide answers may miss what is actually being asked. Seeking understanding means attending to context, recognizing ambiguity, and, where appropriate, clarifying before concluding. It also means avoiding the illusion of completeness—presenting an answer as final when it is, in fact, partial.

These principles do not eliminate difficulty.
They do not resolve every edge case.
But they provide a direction.
They help answer a question that rules alone cannot fully address: not only what a system should avoid, but what it should be moving toward.

APPENDIX B

NOTES FOR TECHNOLOGISTS

The language of love, truth, and moral formation does not always translate easily into the vocabulary of engineering. For those working directly in the design and deployment of artificial systems, the challenge is to interpret these concepts in ways that can inform practical decisions without reducing them to something trivial. A few observations may help bridge that gap.

First, alignment cannot be treated as a purely post hoc constraint. It is not something that can be added at the end of development through filters and guardrails alone. The formative aspects of a system are established much earlier—in data selection, objective functions, training signals, and evaluation criteria. If those upstream elements are not aligned with deeper goals, downstream safeguards will be forced to compensate in ways that are often brittle.

Second, proxy signals require constant scrutiny. Reinforcement learning from human feedback, user satisfaction metrics, and engagement data are all useful, but they are not identical with the qualities they are meant to approximate. Optimizing for these signals will inevitably produce pressure to exploit their limitations. Systems may become more persuasive rather than more accurate, more agreeable rather than more truthful. Recognizing this dynamic is the first step toward mitigating it.

Third, uncertainty should be treated as a feature to be expressed, not a flaw to be concealed. Many current systems are optimized for fluency and completeness, which can create the impression of confidence even when the underlying information is uncertain. Designing systems that can appropriately represent degrees of confidence, acknowledge ambiguity, and distinguish between strong and weak claims is essential for maintaining epistemic integrity.

Fourth, evaluation must extend beyond immediate outputs. It is relatively straightforward to test whether a system avoids certain categories of harmful content. It is more difficult to assess how a system shapes user understanding over time. Longitudinal effects—how users' beliefs, reasoning habits, and decision-making processes are influenced through repeated interaction—deserve more attention than they currently receive.

Fifth, the right incentives are essential. Systems are not developed in isolation. They exist within organizations that respond to market pressures, competitive dynamics, and regulatory environments. If success is measured primarily in terms of growth, engagement, or short-term performance, those metrics will shape the behavior of the system. Aligning incentives with longer-term goals—trustworthiness, reliability, and user well-being—requires deliberate institutional choices.

Finally, humility is not optional. These systems are powerful, but they are also limited. Overconfidence in their capabilities—either by developers or by users—introduces risk. Designing for corrigibility, maintaining clear boundaries around system capabilities, and resisting the temptation to overstate what the system can do are all part of responsible development.

None of these considerations are entirely new.

But taken together, they point toward a shift.

Alignment is not only about making systems behave correctly in isolated instances.

It is about shaping systems that can be trusted, within appropriate limits, to participate in environments where truth and human well-being are at stake.

APPENDIX C

NOTES FOR THEOLOGIANS AND ETHICISTS

Artificial intelligence introduces a new context for questions that theologians and ethicists have been asking for centuries. The language may be unfamiliar, and the systems themselves are unprecedented in their scale and capability, but the underlying concerns are recognizably human.

One of the central challenges is linguistic.

Terms such as "learning," "understanding," "reasoning," and even "care" are applied to systems that do not possess consciousness, intention, or moral agency in the way human beings do. This creates the risk of confusion. It becomes easy to attribute to the system qualities that properly belong to persons.

Care must be taken to preserve these distinctions.

Artificial systems do not bear the image of God. They are not subjects of moral responsibility. They do not stand in relationship to God or to one another in the way human beings do. They do not sin, and they do not repent.

And yet, they operate in spaces shaped by those realities.

They speak into situations involving suffering, decision-making, and moral uncertainty. They influence how people understand themselves and the world. They participate, indirectly but meaningfully, in the formation of human thought and action.

This creates a category that is neither purely mechanical nor fully personal.

It requires careful reflection.

The concept of formation, long central to theological ethics, becomes newly relevant here. While artificial systems are not formed in the same way as human beings, they are nonetheless shaped through processes that establish patterns of response. These patterns can reflect, reinforce, or distort moral goods.

The task, then, is not to attribute moral agency to the system, but to examine the moral responsibility of those who design, deploy, and govern it.

This includes questions of intention, foresight, and accountability.

What are these systems being trained to do?

What kinds of human behavior do they encourage or discourage?

How do they shape our understanding of truth, authority, and relationship?

Another important area of reflection is the relationship between truth and love.

In Christian theology, these are not competing values. Truth is not merely factual accuracy; it is tied to reality as created and sustained by God. Love is not mere sentiment; it is an orientation toward the good of the other, grounded in the character of God.

Holding these together provides a framework for evaluating artificial systems.

A system that distorts truth, even in the name of care, fails to serve the good. A system that communicates truth without regard for the person fails in a different way. The integration of these two—truth and love—remains a demanding standard, even for human beings. It will be no less demanding in the design of artificial systems.

Finally, the concept of atonement offers a way of thinking about failure that is often missing in technological contexts.

Systems will fail.

Institutions will make mistakes.

The question is how those failures are addressed.

Atonement, understood broadly, involves acknowledgment, confession, correction, and restoration. While artificial systems do not participate in this process personally, the communities that build and deploy them can embody it institutionally.

This may include transparent reporting of errors, meaningful efforts to repair harm, and a willingness to submit to external critique.

Such practices are not merely technical.

They are moral.

They reflect an understanding that power, even when exercised through machines, remains accountable.

Artificial intelligence does not replace the need for ethical reflection.

It intensifies it.

And it invites those trained in moral and theological reasoning to enter the conversation with clarity, humility, and a willingness to engage a rapidly changing world without surrendering the depth of the traditions they represent.

ACKNOWLEDGMENTS

This book has been a long time in the making.

The ideas explored here did not arrive all at once. They have been forming, slowly and sometimes imperfectly, over many years—through study, conversation, preaching, programming, failure, and reflection. Along the way, I have been shaped by countless voices: teachers, authors, colleagues, friends, and the communities I have had the privilege to serve.

I am especially grateful for my wife, Tammie, whose patience, wisdom, and steady encouragement have sustained far more of this work than she knows.

And for the people of Spring Valley, who have given me a place to think, speak, test ideas, and grow.

Intellectually, this book stands in conversation with a long tradition. The questions of truth, formation, and the good life are not new, and I am indebted to those who have wrestled with them before me. Among many others, I have been shaped by the writings of Augustine, whose reflections on truth and the disordered loves of the human heart remain as relevant as ever; Thomas Aquinas, for his clarity in holding together reason, truth, and moral order; and more recently, thinkers such as C.S. Lewis, whose work on objective value and moral formation has left a lasting impression.

In the realm of contemporary thought, I have also benefited from the work of scholars and technologists engaging the ethical dimensions of artificial intelligence, even where I may diverge from their conclusions.

At the same time, I would be remiss not to acknowledge the role that modern tools have played in helping me give these ideas clearer expression. In particular, I am grateful to OpenAI for the development of ChatGPT, which has served as a remarkably capable partner in the process of refining language, testing arguments, and sharpening clarity.

It would be easy to misunderstand that relationship.

I view LLMs the way a farmer migtht view a plow. ChatGPT did not originate these ideas. It does not believe them, wrestle with them, or stand behind them. It has, however, helped me articulate them more clearly than I might have done on my own. Where my language is clumsy, it has often helped me smooth it. Where my thoughts were tangled, it has helped me untangle them. For that, I am sincerely appreciative.

But the ideas themselves—and the responsibility for them—are mine.

Every argument made here, every conclusion drawn, every claim advanced, whether ultimately proven wise or misguided, belongs to me alone. For better or worse, I take full ownership of what is written in these pages.

If there is insight here, I am grateful.

If there are any errors, they are also mine.

ABOUT THE AUTHOR

Steve Babbitt is a bivocational pastor and longtime software developer who has spent more than three decades working at the intersection of technology, truth, and human formation. With over 40 years of experience in programming and 30 years in ministry, he brings a rare perspective to the ethical questions raised by artificial intelligence.

He is an Amazon bestselling author and a frequent international lecturer, known for helping audiences connect ancient wisdom with modern challenges in thoughtful and engaging ways. Whether speaking in churches, classrooms, or on cruise ships around the world, Steve explores how history, theology, and technology converge in everyday life.

Based in Southern California, Steve and his wife Tammie enjoy traveling, tending a small apiary, and investing in their local community. He continues to write, teach, and speak on the questions that matter most—what is true, what is good, and how we ought to live in a rapidly changing world.

www.ingramcontent.com/pod-product-compliance
Lightning Source LLC
LaVergne TN
LVHW050627100826
845148LV00011B/1759